The Art of Becoming a Successful & Wealthy Educator in China for Expats

Dr. William Clifton Green II

The Art of Becoming a Successful & Wealthy Educator in China for Expats
Copyright ©2020 by Dr. William Clifton Green II
All Rights Reserved

The Content is for informational purposes only; you should not construe any such information or other material as legal, tax, investment, financial, or other advice. Nothing contained in this book constitutes a solicitation, recommendation, endorsement, or offer by author or publisher. All Content is the information of a general nature and does not address the circumstances of any particular individual or entity. Nothing in the book constitutes professional and/or financial advice, nor does any information in the book constitute a comprehensive or complete statement of the matters discussed or the law relating thereto. You alone assume the sole responsibility of evaluating the merits and risks associated with the use of any information or making any decisions based on such information or other content. You agree not to hold the author or publisher, its affiliates for any possible claim for damages arising from any decision you make based on information available to you through this book. All rights reserved. No part of this publication may be reproduced, distributed, or transmitted in any form or by any means, including photocopying, recording, or other electronic or mechanical methods, without the prior written permission of the AUTHOR, except in the case of brief quotations embodied in critical reviews and certain other noncommercial uses permitted by copyright law.

Publisher: Absolute Author Publishing House
Editor: Dr. Melissa Caudle
Cover Designer:

Paperback ISBN: 978-1-64953-097-4
eBook ISBN: 978-1-64953-098-1

1. Teaching 2. Overseas Employment 3. Workforce

Dedication

I dedicate this book to my son and daughter.

Table of Contents

Part 1: The Right Mindset 1
  Introduction..1
  Who Am I?...3
  The Post Pandemic World 6
  You Must Get Qualified To Teach At Elite Schools In China 9
  Why Should I Come to China? 11
  What Is the Right Mindset? 17
  Summary..32

Part 2: Getting Ready 36
  Qualifications Needed...36
  Types of Teaching-related Opportunities 42
  Avoid making these mistakes 57
  Summary..61

Part 3: Success in the Classroom 65
  Overview to Success in Teaching 68
  Putting Theory Into Practice 72
  In Class Teaching Tips and Guidelines 80
  Office Communication..84

Summary 92
Part 4: How to Make a Passive Income in Education...96
How to Profit In The Field Of Education 100
Respect your School and Respect the Law 107
Where Do I Go from Here? 107
Summary 110

Part 1: The Right Mindset
Introduction

This book was written during the height of the COVID-19 pandemic. Economies around the world are facing setbacks at an unprecedented level. Many of these economies will remain in stagnation and decline into the foreseeable future. It seems that every day on the news, one can hear about the latest corporation struggling or going bankrupt. Highly qualified and educated people no longer have the luxury of choosing white-collar jobs. In desperation, many are applying to work at restaurants and supermarkets, places where their credentials make them vastly over-qualified. People with PhDs around the world are applying for jobs at Dunkin Donuts. If that sounds like the situation you are currently faced with, know that you are not alone. You also need to know that there is another way to success if you're patient, willing to work, and to grow.

My base of operation is in Shanghai, China, where I have resided for the past ten years. Lockdown has ended here, and there is no longer a need to self-quarantine. Life has gone back to normal, for the most part. This year is certainly one where many new social distancing customs have become more and more commonplace for everyone. People wear surgical masks when they go out. I certainly wear my face mask when going out and make sure to equally ensure that my hands are properly sanitized when I go indoors. I assume that wearing face masks will be a custom that is going to stay with humanity in the far future.

The current situation in the wider world, though it is still one of desperation. People in many countries are not sure what next year will be like. World economies have taken a turn for the worse. Businesses, large and small, are closing. The outlook, for the most part, seems bleak. Cases of the virus are spiking in some countries. In other countries, leaders are considering closing down again after having previously decided to reopen their countries to internal and external travel. People are unsure of whether to travel long distances or stay in their local communities.

Despite these very real concerns, I am optimistic about the future. One reason for writing this book is to provide a sense of hope. Indeed, the world is becoming a smaller and smaller place. Opportunities for international exchange and cooperation are certainly going to increase. They must if we are to endure and once again thrive. I predict that the area where we have the most opportunity for making the world a better place is through education. Nowhere will this be more apparent than in China.

China has over 1.3 billion people and high demand for expats to teach English, among other subjects, through the medium of the English language. Teaching and leadership positions in education come with high salaries, premium insurance packages, and generous housing allowances. There is a plethora of teaching opportunities that are available to those who have put in the groundwork to get qualified and know how to develop positive, rewarding careers. The problem is that most do not know where to start in order to take advantage of these wonderful opportunities.

The purpose of this book is to shed light on that process providing clarity in terms of how to thrive in the golden age of China. Thus, there is hope, especially for those who want to pursue a career in the field of education in China. Let me reiterate that the demand for educators is still extraordinarily strong, and you can be one of them. In this book, I will teach you how to develop the right mindset, get the right credentials, and achieve success in the classroom as well as professionally. Finally, I am going to give you the steps I took to become an educator in China. Before I go any further, let me introduce myself.

Who Am I?

I am Dr. William Clifton Green II, and I have been involved in education in China for the past ten years and education in general, for the past seventeen years. I have served as Academic Quality Manager, Curriculum Coordinator at a well-known international school as well as co-founder of a language training center. My experiences in China have primarily been in Shanghai, although I did complete an internship at an education start up for three months in Beijing in 2009. You should also know that I am a Black American from the state of South Carolina. Indeed, while many have expressed otherwise vis-à-vis the Black experience overseas, I believe that I have achieved a great deal in spite of being an ethnic minority living overseas. Furthermore, in the long run, having more challenges actually prompted me to make the necessary decisions and sacrifices that led to the breakthroughs that would come later.

In 2015, I acquired a house in Shanghai. In 2017, I bought an imported BMW SUV. For those of you who don't know, property in Shanghai is vastly expensive, and the property that I initially acquired for $500,000 is now valued at $1,500,000. Most recently, I completed my doctorate in Educational Leadership and Management with a specialization in Administration and accepted a leadership position at a famous international school. I tell you these things not to make you feel discouraged, nor do I wish to appear braggadocios. I tell you these things to inspire you to begin your journey. I want you to achieve your purpose in life. If a man from rural South Carolina who had few resources can overcome and achieve against all odds, you most certainly can as well.

I developed my love for teaching when I was in Japan from 2005-early 2008. I primarily worked as an Assistant Language Teacher (ALT) in primary school during that time and also worked part-time for adult language schools and study abroad centers. It was during this time that I received positive feedback from one of my employers who inspired me to pursue and further develop my career in education. He told me that I was a good teacher and that education was the right field for me. Inspired by his feedback, I completed my master's degree in TESOL/Applied Linguistics at Columbia University. After graduating from Columbia, I decided to move to Shanghai, China, to start my professional career in education.

I founded a language training center that serves students aged three to fourteen years old and worked as a Curriculum Coordinator at an international school. During this time, I also completed my online teaching certification. I became a licensed teacher in Washington, DC, with a specialization in K-12 and English as a Second Language (ESL). My motivation for completing the teaching certification was that I had just entered the international school. Still, I was unable to teach in the international stream as a teacher since I didn't have a teaching license.

It was during my online teaching practicum, where I learned from an advisor that one thing was missing from my academic credentials -- a doctorate in Leadership. Thus, in 2016, I entered the doctoral program at Drexel University online and successfully defended my dissertation in February 2020. During this time, the number of students at the center grew from eight to 550 students at the time that this book was written. These experiences have shaped my understanding of the field of education as well as how one might be successful in the industry. As such, in this book, I intend to show you how you can use online tools, professional connections, and time-proven strategies to become a successful educator in China.

The Post Pandemic World

Let's fast forward slightly to the beginning of the pandemic. In February, many in the educational industry thought the pandemic would be over in a couple of months, and many decided to offer online classes for free during the quarantine. I anticipated the worst and had my teachers commit fully online teaching with the understanding that the situation would not be improving anytime into the far future. We created an online curriculum and a system for storing online assessments. Furthermore, we informed parents that online classes would cost the same as offline classes. Three months later, training centers near us were regretting their decision as they understood that we were in a pandemic situation, and children would not be allowed to return to school anytime soon. Thus, they were losing money. Although the education industry remained relatively stable, my point is that it always pays to be proactive and prepared for the worst.

Remember the story about the ant and the grasshopper. The ant worked hard to store food for the winter. He was worried about the future and, in particular, the bitter cold was a stern warning that forebode the impending coming of death, melancholy, and insecurity. Visualizing this fate, he worked ever so hard during the summer and autumn, gathering what resources he could, all the while knowing what would happen. The grasshopper meanwhile dithered here and there while living precariously in the moment. He never thought of what would come when the world became dark, empty, and frigid beyond all belief. He relied solely on his privilege and friendships. And as the story goes, these were not enough to save him. When winter came, he had nothing, and there was no one who could save him from his fate.

We are living in such a world today. In many ways, the pandemic has been like winter for many of us. It has taught us how to save. It has taught us how to be resourceful. It has taught us to have the foresight and to be ready for the next impending coming of doom. Indeed, so long as our genetic makeup exists in the world so that disease will accompany us. It is up to us to take the proper precautions to safeguard our futures and legacies. It is no longer sufficient to depend on privilege alone to progress in a world where large companies are going bankrupt, economies are stagnant, and hope simply means surviving.

What if I were to tell you that during the pandemic, I made more money than I did before the start of the pandemic? Would you believe me? It is true. The reason is that unlike others; I had no privilege to rely on, ever. One of my teachers once said to me, "William, I don't have to worry too much. I have white privilege, so the parents will always like me." Yes, he actually said that to me, his boss. And actually, once upon a time, he would have been absolutely right. But today, he is wrong. In a growing world of insecurity where parents' incomes are affected by the pandemic, several parents have requested that their children leave their class for a better teacher from Jamaica. In difficult situations, privilege flies out of the window. The conversation shifts from what you are potentially worth to what you can actually do. In this climate of uncertainty, the conversation changes from the hypothetical to the practical. These days, people desperately need results. During the pandemic, when there was a shortage of teachers, I was given opportunities because I was the highest qualified in this field. That's how I was able to make more money during the pandemic than before it. I wasn't always so fortunate.

When the economy was good in the early 2000s, and I was younger, life was difficult. I applied for teaching opportunities and could only acquire some opportunities. I recall seeing some job opportunities that specifically stated that the school or employer was only looking for White teachers or "European" teachers, which oddly meant White as well. The qualification of the teacher was secondary to his or her race, generally speaking. You wouldn't believe me if I told you that I remember, when I lived in Japan, walking into a school and there were a bunch of Black Sambo dolls at the front desk, and I was greeted by a White American interviewer who decided not to give me the job for some reason. I wonder why not?

There, of course, were some exceptions, and these are places where I worked. I worked at schools, and I had to prove myself to the management constantly. And I did because, like the ant, I needed to survive. I worked overtime. I prepared for classes well, and I treated each child or adult I taught with the utmost respect. They were my lifeline. Also, I grew to like teaching very much. The management teams around me were also giving me positive feedback regarding how students viewed my classes and me.

On the other hand, I knew that I couldn't continue working for mediocre pay or working seven days a week without moving up into leadership and management. I had no idea about investments or real estate in my twenties, but instinctively felt that the status quo was not going to get me anywhere. So, I decided to complete my master's degree in TESOL and Applied Linguistics at Columbia University. I always wanted to study at an Ivy League institution to further my education. The experience gave me an immense advantage in the field. I learned how to write course curricula and lesson plans, how to assess students during class properly, and how to collaborate with other teachers.

Education, for me, was like a vaccine against the pandemic of racism and discrimination in the workplace. All of a sudden, after graduating, I have widely been sought after. Schools that I had applied to begin contacting me. Of course, this didn't mean that racism disappeared per se. It just means that, on paper, the Columbia degree made my application stand out, which means that I had more opportunities to get in front of the interviewers. I went on to become a certified IELTS examiner as well as complete my doctorate to remain relevant. And it has paid off. Throughout this book, I will continually stress the importance of upgrading one's qualifications as a means of advancement and improving one's life. It just makes economic sense to invest in an educational degree and enter the profession in China, particularly in a post-pandemic world. For those wishing to enter the educational profession in China, it is an absolute must.

You Must Get Qualified to Teach at Elite Schools in China

China has recently made it clear that unqualified teachers will not be allowed to teach there. For example, all teachers who are sponsored on a Z work visa must now have their academic credentials notarized and authenticated by the person's local consulate or embassy in China or the Chinese embassy in their respective countries. In addition, teachers must provide a notarized and authenticated background check as well to prove that they don't have a criminal record back in their respective countries. Finally, some regions have even specified a certain number of years that a foreigner needs to have taught to get a visa. For example, Beijing requires that a teacher have at least five years of teaching experience.

The reason for these requirements is obvious. In the past, teachers could rely on their expat privilege to secure a job. Oftentimes, these teachers were under-qualified or not qualified at all. Some teachers landed nice jobs at universities with fake degrees. I know several teachers who did this. One woman, in particular, was teaching at a prestigious school where the tuition was well over 20,000 USD a year, and she barely graduated from high school. Recently though, as a result of the new policy changes, teachers, such as the woman above, no longer have teaching positions and have had to look for employment elsewhere. It's really unfortunate because I distinctly remember telling that teacher to get qualified on multiple occasions. Had she done an online degree program from a reputable university with the money that she was making, she would have still been able to continue her teaching career. As I said, I was spared through all of this as I had all of my qualifications in order and, like the ant, was prepared for any eventuality. You must remember that I was competing against the odds, perhaps just as you are today, but there is hope so long as one is willing to work for it.

As we enter a new era, the days of privilege are over, and the COVID outbreak has sounded the death knell on the notion that one can treat teaching in China as a gap year or backpacking affair. For one, parents are demanding that teachers get results to a greater degree than before. Parents are keen to ask questions about teachers' qualifications and backgrounds. As people begin tightening their belts in light of a less financially secure world, they will inevitably become more and more scrupulous about how and where they invest their hard-earned money. Education is greatly valued in China, which is why I believe you should come to look for opportunities. There will certainly be a plethora of opportunities into the far future. On the other hand, you have to come with the right mindset, which is the focus of the next section.

Why Should I Come to China?

I have lived in China for a decade. The country, culture, and people are mesmerizing, and the transformation of the country has been phenomenal. In 2006, I visited China for the first time. I took a train from Shanghai to Xining, Qinghai, which is the province above Tibet. There was construction everywhere, and the trains were slow. Fast forward to 2020, and the country has been modernized in many regards. There are skyscrapers, subway stations, and bullet trains throughout the country. Many rest stops in suburban areas have Starbucks, and cash is rarely used anymore. Almost everyone uses their phones, which are ubiquitous in the major cities and villages, to pay for everything.

I have often reflected on the appeal of China in the modern age. There are currently hundreds of thousands of expats living here, and more will surely come as China's economy develops in the coming decade. When it comes to the field of education, it's important that more highly qualified teachers come here to take advantage of the vast number of opportunities for high paying salaries and career development. Thus, if you were to ask me if you should come to China, I would definitely say yes. In addition, I could give you three reasons why you should come instantly off the top of my head: food and drink, cultural diversity, and opportunities for career development.

1. **Food and Drink** - Everyone knows about the popularity of Chinese food. You will probably see me make mention of Chinese food several times in this book. In my hometown in South Carolina, we don't have a McDonalds, but we have a Chinese food restaurant. Yet, nothing compares with the variety of authentic Chinese food in China. The diversity of the food is vast as the country itself.

   Personally, I prefer the northwestern style of food with its mutton dishes, noodles, and dairy products. Particularly in places such as Qinghai and Inner Mongolia, you can enjoy tender meat that falls off the bone as you pick it up with your hands. Northwesterners also like to eat lamb kebabs, which are flavored with cumin powder. Yak meat is popular in some regions in the west. Also, while traveling around Qinghai, one can find freshly made yogurt everywhere. In Xinjiang, you can try a mutton pilaf, which is very scrumptious.

   And then there are times when I prefer the cuisine of Xi'an, home of the famous Terra Cotta Warriors. Personally, I think Xi'an food is spicy and filling. There are a lot of flour-based foods from Xi'an, but I especially like Youpo noodles, which come in a red, spicy soup, and dumplings, which also have a similarly stimulating sauce. Dumplings, in general, are always good, and the stuffing for the dumplings is becoming more and more creative. Liangpi, which is also served with Xi'an food, is always a treat. Liangpi is often translated as cold noodles, and while it is not typically served hot, it is sometimes transparent and thicker than your average order of noodles.

If you are looking for a taste of Panda express, China mainland style, here are some similarities I have found. Sweet and sour dishes are very similar to what you can get back home in terms of flavor. Kung Pao chicken, which is pronounced *"gōng bǎo jī dīng"* in Chinese, is unbelievably delicious with a thicker and richer sauce than its cousin back home. Egg rolls can be found in every city. Fried rice is good as well, but it's usually served in large portions and typically best enjoyed with two or more people, especially if you're on a diet. As for fortune cookies, I haven't seen them around, and they seem to be an anomaly to most Chinese people. I have seen one once in a restaurant in Shanghai, which was supposed to be like a Panda Express for the expat community. That's right. It was a restaurant serving Westernized Chinese food to expats in China.

There are other local cuisines such as Yunnan food, Shanghai-style food with the most famous dish being *xiaolongbao*, a kind of steamed bun, Hong Kong-style food, and Sichuan food, which is famed for being the spiciest Chinese food. The list goes on and on. Every region has its own special variety of food, herbs, spices, and methods of preparation. To be honest, even after ten years, I have barely scratched the surface in terms of uncovering all the Chinese cuisines. Many Chinese people feel the same. In a culinary sense, China is a country with a wide range of scrumptious delights that always keeps one's taste buds engaged.

This means when you come here, you will have more than enough dishes to satiate your appetite. And if this wasn't enough, in recent years, there has been a trend of fusion restaurants that combine old and new, reinterpret classical dishes as well as create novel, regional combinations (i.e., Northwestern, and European styles). One such restaurant is called Xibe, which is located in Shanghai. It's a blend of the culinary styles of the Xibe people of Xinjiang with a modern European twist. So, for example, you can find mutton and cheese buns on the menu.

Coffee is also readily available, even in smaller towns. Most major cities have cafes on nearly every block. Starbucks is the most common Western café, but one can also find Costa coffee as well. Local companies have sprung up in recent years and offer varying degrees of quality. Quite a few have reached a high level in terms of the quality of the coffee as well as customer service such as Manner coffee.

Finally, of course, what you will find in China in recent times is the introduction of Western food. Milk, butter, cheese, and spaghetti are readily available in supermarkets. Peanut butter and jelly, Nutella, Corn Flakes, and steak can also be easily found in the city. There is a cornucopia of Western restaurants in all major cities such as McDonald's, Burger King, and cafes such as Starbucks. There are numerous Italian restaurants, Japanese Izakayas and Teppanyaki, and Korean barbecue restaurants. One can even find Mongolian and Jamaican restaurants in the major cities. The variety of food is stunning and simply amazing. If you like good food, you should definitely come to China.

2. **Cultural Diversity** - China has many ethnic and ethnolinguistic groups. Diversity means that there is so much to learn. Currently, I am learning Shanghainese and most recently realized that there are sub-dialects in Shanghai, such as the dialect spoken in the Jinshan region. These dialects in China are sometimes mutually intelligible with Mandarin and for expats, studying a dialect is really like studying another language. You can also learn other languages and experience differing ethnic groups as well. For example, in inner Mongolian, you can learn Mongolian or Evenki if you so desired. In Qinghai or Tibet, you could learn Tibetan. In the northeast, you could learn Manchu from the Manchurians. In the northeast, you could potentially study Korean to speak with the Korean ethnic minority or learn Russian.

3. There are fifty-six ethnic groups in China. Each ethnic group has its traditions and cultures as well as languages and/or dialects. So, in addition to the

differing regional patterns of food, dress, and traditions, ethnic groups also have their diversity in these areas, which means you will have a lot to learn. I recently took an interest in the horse head fiddle, which is played by the ethnic Mongolians. When you arrive, you will undoubtedly become fascinated by some aspect of China's diverse culture and people.

China's cultural diversity and varied climate and environment go hand in hand. In the far north, it is cold. Still, you can enjoy ice sculptures in places such as Harbin in the winter, or you can go down to Sanya on Hainan island in the winter to enjoy late spring-like twenty-five-degree tropical weather and go snorkeling and eat guava. You can climb mountains in Anhui province or visit rice paddies and ferry down rivers in Guangxi province and explore villages of the Zhuang people. The stunning variety is mindboggling, and this makes China an ideal place to live and learn about their people, food, and culture.

4. **Career Opportunities** - Last but not least, the most important reason to come to China is for career opportunities. China has over 1.3 billion people, and foreigners make a small fraction of this population. There is currently a demand for foreigners in the field of education across the country. I am willing to wager that 100% of all qualified expat teachers who arrive and have read this book can and will be able to find full-time high paying employment. This is a *sine qua non* as the demand for qualified and professional educators vastly exceeds the current supply.

5. Knowing that there is a huge demand for language teaching and education for expats should excite and motivate you. Particularly if you are currently living in an area where opportunities are sparse. Know that an online course or a TESL certification can mean the difference between working for minimum wage at McDonald's or Dunkin Donuts and making 50,000 USD a year. Again, I am not knocking working at McDonald's or Dunkin Donuts, but if you want to make more, then you are going to have to go where the grass is greener. And China can potentially be that place.

What Is the Right Mindset?

Getting in the right mindset happens long before you book the air ticket to travel overseas. I have lived almost 40% of my life overseas: four years in Japan, ten years in China, and half a year in Britain and France. I have passed the Japanese and Chinese language proficiency exams. I have seen many expats come and go. I have also noticed some winning patterns among the more successful expats in the field of education, particularly those who stayed long term and made teaching a career. Keep in mind that this mindset begins as soon as you decide that you want to begin teaching in China. These are ten principles or guidelines for developing the right mindset that will help you to get on the right course toward success if you plan to teach in China:

1. **Having an Abundance Mindset** - The advantages of living in abundance are life-changing. First of all,

you get more respect when you are in a position where there is a considerable demand for your skill or trade. The desire for qualified teachers is the reason I was able to keep my head above water and thrive during the Coronavirus pandemic. No matter what happened, I knew there were opportunities available. In addition, you, living in abundance, gives you the confidence to access your unlimited potential. Once I had secured my teaching job in China using my master's degree, I was promoted. I then began the process of getting my K-12 teaching certification and then my doctorate after that. In the meantime, I created an app for the iPhone. The momentum was exhilarating and was the result of living in abundance. Finally, the result of living in abundance is that you can maintain your health and well-being. When you know that more success is coming your way, you feel better, more energetic, and willing to make your place in the world.

If, until now, you haven't felt as excited about your current situation, I wholeheartedly recommend researching career opportunities in China and then preparing for your trip. Having this mindset is critical to undertaking the necessary requirements below that will propel you to a successful career in education. It is the first step to developing a career that will be worthwhile in an ever-changing, increasingly unpredictable world.

2. **It's Important to Learn the Local Language And Culture.** - This has got to be very obvious. You need to learn, at least, a basic level of Chinese and not for

teaching purposes but to be able to communicate with the people in supermarkets, at the bank, or in the queue at the subway station. I recommend investing in a beginning level Chinese language book. It doesn't matter which publisher you go with, but there are some recommendations that I have learned over the years.

A) The book should contain explanations behind the grammar. Although Chinese is a subject-object-verb language like English, it also has topic-comment constructions. Books that clearly explain the grammatical differences between English and Chinese go a long way in terms of helping you master the language.

B) The vocabulary should be relevant and simple. Choose books that have the normal everyday vocabulary. For example, you probably need to know the word "restroom," "卫生间 or *wèi shēng jiān*," and not the word "phoenix," "凤凰," or "*fèng huáng*." A simple flip through the textbook will reveal if the book is of an appropriate level and if the content will help you get around during your first week in China. Again, the critical thing is being able to get around once you arrive.

C) Phrase books are also useful, as memorizing chunks of language can help you if you get in a difficult situation. For example, "I want a taxi to go to the airport." "我需要一辆出租车去机场" "Wǒ xū yào yī liàng chū zū chē qù jī cháng."

D) Avoid books, at least for the time being, that teach archaic or ancient information which could be useful on an intellectual level, but won't help you when you desperately need it at the restaurant when you need to tell the waiter to split the bill.

It's also important to learn about the culture. The Chinese culture has been described as collectivist or group minded in nature. I would say yes and no to that type of generalization. Yes, it is collectivist if you consider the fact that family meals are typically had in a communal fashion where people eat from the same dishes. And many people also use apps such as TikTok to express their individuality and uniqueness. Also, younger people have characteristics that differ significantly from the older generation, having grown up in a time of relative prosperity and historically unprecedented levels of familial support. I could go on and on, but understanding a culture involves more than reading about it or generalizing it with platitudinous terms. It is through interaction that you gain insight into a culture and its people. You can begin this process even before you set foot in another country.

I recall when I was learning Japanese many years ago at Columbia University, I had few opportunities to practice back in the United States. So, what I did was go around the university campus. When I heard someone speaking Japanese, I would go to them and practice speaking. I found that people were very happy when I did this and were willing to invite me into their group. I made quite a few Japanese friends that way. I also joined the Friends of Japan Club that met weekly on campus, which gave me more opportunities to practice.

Joining language groups online or offline can help you improve your cultural knowledge. I recommend such groups as they provide insight into a culture in a way that books or superficial knowledge cannot. In sum, it's one thing to talk about a culture, and it's another actually to experience it. I recommend that you come and experience Chinese culture for yourself.

3. **Make Sure You Understand Your Language and Culture.** - Quick. What part of speech is the word "likely?" What kind of sentence is this? "John gave me a book because I asked him for it." Or why is it so difficult to understand Beowulf? Before coming to China, you need to review the parts of speech and the basic rules about grammar. It doesn't matter if you come to China to be a history teacher or mathematics teacher, reviewing English grammar before you come to China will be key. The reason for this is that most of your students will be non-native speaking students, even if you teach at an international school. In addition, if you are not good at spelling, now is a good time to review basic

spelling. I can't tell you how many times I've been asked to spell words, and I've seen teachers sometimes make the most mundane spelling mistakes.

When I say learn your own culture, I mean you should know about the region in which you come from. For example, what is your regional bird or flower? What landmarks are famous in your hometown, and why? For you, this may seem mundane, but for your students and colleagues in China, these topics will make great conversation starters and be the source of much intrigue. In truth, I have learned more about my home state during my time in China than I did when I was stateside. I recommend learning beforehand and also preparing any realia or other items of note to bring to show colleagues and students after you have arrived.

4. **It's Necessary to Get Your Teaching or Educational Credentials Beforehand, If Possible.** - While I intend to devote a section of this book to how you can obtain your teaching certification online, I will say that it is better if you can do so before you come to China, and the reason is simple. International schools often offer better packages to qualified teachers who they can recruit from overseas. Such packages include a generous housing and relocation allowance. If you are interested in how to get your teaching certification, check out Chapter 4.

If you are attending a university, I believe any educational degree will be an advantage. Majors such as education, leadership, English, mathematics, and so are good. The School of Education at many universities has extended programs where students not only receive a degree but also get support with obtaining their teaching certification at graduation. That was one mistake I made. Columbia University, Teachers College offered a path to get the teaching license and certification in the state of New York. However, I took the route of only getting my master's degree. That meant that I didn't get my teaching certification until after I had arrived in China. It will always work out in your favor to get your teaching certification before going to China.

Another credential that I think helps is obtaining a first aid certification. This is a skill set that is valuable anywhere on the planet when it comes to saving the lives of others. If you have a talent for playing the piano or guitar, getting a certification would also be beneficial as many schools highly value teachers with academic as well as extracurricular skills. Finally, if you can take the Chinese proficiency exam known as the HSK, the letters of the acronym stand for Chinese Proficiency Exam, in Chinese, that would be very useful. There are six levels of this exam, with level 1 being the most elementary level and level 6 being the most advanced. I have passed level 5 and currently studying to pass level 6. In my opinion, anything over level 4 is intended for those who intend to study at university or live long term. In the beginning and if you are still in your home country, make passing the lower levels first your main goal. Choosing an exam to prepare for is excellent because you will have specific content to study, and your study progression will move in a stepwise manner.

I also recommend that a teacher read books on human psychology if not minor in the subject at school. Knowing human psychology is essential for connecting with people as well as understanding their desires and aspirations. I majored in psychology in undergrad, and it helped me better understand the intrinsic or internal as well as the extrinsic or external motivations driving my students' and colleagues' unique behaviors. Having a grounding in psychology will also help you to understand yourself better as you navigate the cross-cultural landscape that you will find yourself in when you move to China.

Again, all of these credentials are necessary for ensuring that you hit the ground running and will help make your resume more stellar and appealing to schools and other academic institutions in China. Having a teaching certification gives you the advantage of getting access to high-paying jobs. Having solid Chinese skills could potentially open the door to leadership opportunities where you need to work with Chinese as well as Western staff. However, as I will allude to later in this book, the process of career and professional development is ongoing, and you should strive to continue this process after you have arrived in China.

5. **Getting Teaching Experience at Home Is Key.** - In addition to academic qualifications, you will need to

obtain some experience teaching. If you're a student on campus, you can volunteer to tutor one-to-one if you're not enrolled in a Department of Education program. If you're enrolled in a degree in the Department of Education, you should be able to complete a teaching practicum. If you're not on campus, volunteering at a local school and becoming involved in student learning are key to learning how to become an educator. To my mind, the successful educator is not only a person knowledgeable of a particular subject but also one who can connect with students on a humanistic level, showing concern and empathy for the unique individual's needs and, at the same time, make the learning experience pedagogically meaningful and motivating. This is a unique balance of skills the professional educator possesses, which only emerge after many years of observation and careful practice.

If you're new to the field, just think back to your favorite teacher in school. He or she was probably not only knowledgeable of the subject being taught but was also interesting and exciting to listen to as well. That person probably made you want to focus on the subject at hand. Now, think of that educator who had the opposite effect on you. That is the difference between the teacher who has conscientiously learned to have an impact on students' lives and a teacher who only knows how to relay subject matter knowledge. This is why it's important to observe teaching as much as possible so that you can differentiate between good and bad teaching.

6. **Health Is Essential If You Plan to Live Overseas.**
- One of the reasons why you should go to China is to experience real Chinese food. I plan on delving deep into this topic in later chapters. However, if you suffered from the freshman fifteen, nothing will prepare you for what's coming after you arrive here. The food is good, and, as a guest at your new school, you will be treated to a copious amount of it. You have to prepare yourself for this experience.

I remember my first week in China. I was invited to Xining City in Qinghai province. I was given the guest's welcome with a hodgepodge of local northwestern dishes, mainly consisting of mutton, dairy products such as yogurt followed by beef. There were about six of us in total, but the table had around fifteen or more dishes. Being from the South in the USA, I was raised to believe that it is polite to finish all the food at the table to show respect to the preparers of the meal. Anyhow, long story short, no matter how much I tried to finish the food, the dishes kept coming, and no longer how hard I tried to finish Qinghai style liquor, the glasses kept being refilled. Little did I know at the time that my best course of action in this culture would have been to stop eating and drinking. This is because in Chinese culture, to stop consumption means that one's appetite is sated. On the other hand, continuing to eat or drink means that one hasn't had his or her fill.

Needless to say, I gained a lot of weight by eating too much after I arrived in China. The food was just too good. For those of you who have never tried authentic Chinese food, you're in for a treat when you arrive here. It's a thousand-fold better than the Panda Express that you've been frequenting back home. However, you're going to need to have a set exercise routine to keep yourself fit. I didn't get started on a fitness program until after I arrived and joined a gym. You can save yourself the heartache of the gym by establishing a healthy exercise regimen in advance of your arrival. Deciding when you will go for a run, how many pushups and sit-ups you will do a day, as well as how many calories you're comfortably consuming are key to maintaining a healthy lifestyle. It will also help you to gain mental clarity and keep your life in balance, which will also help you to overcome stress as you transition from one culture to another.

7. **Know Thyself.** - The education profession involves interacting with others. You have to decide before you come to China, whether you prefer teaching large groups, small groups, or one to one. Are you more comfortable teaching adults, teenagers, primary school students, or children in a nursery? It's important to think about these questions beforehand because this will help you narrow down your choices when it comes to picking the right school, institution, or training center. That said, you should also decide whether you prefer working for a large organization with thousands of people, medium-size organizations with hundreds of people, or small organizations. Or perhaps you prefer working on one to one as a consultant. There are a variety of factors

that will influence your decision, such as personality type (i.e., are you introverted or extroverted), working style as well as desired or expected salary.

Taking type to reflect on the aforementioned questions will help you to make the best decisions. Equally, you must be able to justify why you prefer such teaching situations and environments. This is why I recommend keeping a journal or diary to record your answers and self-reflections. This will be useful in helping you develop clarity of purpose. Additionally, this will come in handy when you go to interviews. When the interviewee asks you why you prefer to teach younger children, you will be able to respond at length because you have already thought amply about your rationale, purpose, and career direction.

8. **Get in The Habit of Socializing.** - Living in another country means having to build your network from scratch. Most often than not, you will arrive in China without any relatives or contacts other than your new employer. As such, you will need to get connected. If you have been a hermit, you had better change your mindset. If you haven't arrived in China yet, try going outdoors and socializing. Try striking up conversations with people to get new insights. For example, you might point to some frangipani on the windowsill at the florist and inquire as to how to grow such a plant. Or perhaps, ask an engineer how do they know that buildings they build won't fall. Inquiring into the unknown is beneficial for your trip to China as when you arrive, you will find that a lot

is unknown. The culture will be new. The food will be new. I recommend you get in the habit of embracing the unknown and being inquisitive to understand it rather than living in a closed knit social bubble isolated from the vibrant world around you.

In China, apps such as WeChat are critical for socializing and making friends. Using WeChat makes life a whole lot easier. The app interface allows you to add users, share photos and videos of your moments, as well as chat, individually video or voice call or voice message the users that you have added or subsequently communicate in groups of users (up to 500 in total) around some specific topic (e.g., expat life). Most importantly, the app allows you to connect your bank account, add money, and pay for goods everywhere in China. Personally, I primarily use WeChat for individual, private conversation. My colleagues, business connections, and even plumber are easily accessible via WeChat.

9. **Don't Take Yourself Too Seriously.** - Laughing at oneself is commonplace in Chinese culture and shows that one has reached a level of confidence where he or she is comfortable poking fun at him or herself. This is something that I am continually working on to improve within myself. Being self-conscious or taking oneself too seriously is to take the path of self-defeat. Learning not to take oneself so seriously is the path to ever-increasing self-awareness.

I recently recalled when I was on holiday in Thailand; I was sitting in a bar where the music wasn't particularly interesting. I saw that no one was using the DJ equipment. I had never done that before and decided to give it a try. Lo and behold, I was able to turn a few heads after experimenting for a little while. This then piqued my interest in music a little bit. The point being had I not tried the equipment, I would have never known that there was some interest there.

Now, essentially, I intentionally go out with the purpose of losing face (in a good and morally decent way). I don't mean to insinuate that one goes out with the purpose of getting into trouble. Nowadays, I am interested in learning to dance, although I have no rhythm. I am interested in learning how to play the guitar as well as trying to learn how to play mahjong. In the beginning, I always feel a little awkward and feel like the silliest person in the world. In the end, I am always able to learn more and more about myself. The feeling of trying something new and letting go of the ego is the most self-satisfying things, in my opinion. It fills a void and brings joy. It also unleashes the power of humanity to learn, develop, and grow.

So, if there is something you've never tried, go ahead, and give it a shot. You never know where it might lead you. Also, if you have already purchased a Chinese language book, go ahead, and try practicing a few phrases with real people. At first, your pronunciation might be a little off or nearly incomprehensible, but generally speaking, others will correct you and help you to improve. The more opportunities you give yourself through losing face and overcoming your fear, the better the position you will find yourself in.

10. **Get in The Habit of Sharing.** - It is in Chinese culture to give souvenirs to friends and colleagues after one has traveled on holiday. Normally, food from the area you've been to, such as cookies or dried fruit, will make good souvenirs to share with your friends. Souvenirs can also be used as a kind of social currency when one wants to build relationships or good "*guanxi*" with others. The latter point must be heavily emphasized. People describe the term "*guanxi*" as the complex relationship that one has with others. Building *guanxi* can be described as bestowing favors upon another person in the form of gift-giving, supporting another's work or project, or even accompanying a person to the airport or hospital. Ideally, building *guanxi* should be done solely for the betterment of the individual and his or her closet friends, associates, and society as a whole. Of course, *guanxi* can also be used in social advancement in an informal sense. Well, perhaps this doesn't have to be self-serving in and of itself. As the old saying goes, "Helping others equals helping yourself." In any event, sharing is the key to success in China. To be honest, though, sharing is the key to success everywhere.

11. Amongst educators, every great teacher has a cache of teaching and learning resources. I recall one teacher who later was promoted to a very high

position, eagerly shared his PDF books with the whole team. He apparently stayed up late for over a month, downloading resources that would have been inaccessible to the rest of the team. In the end, his resources helped the entire teaching team succeed, and we were all the better for his generous support. As I said, helping others equals helping yourself, so, whether he knew it or not, that teacher was setting himself up to be promoted.

If you are now asking the question of what you can share as an educator, well, the answer is not as complicated as it may seem. You can share links to websites that you think will be useful in the classroom. You can share your workout routine. You can create a group on WeChat, the Chinese version of What's App, and share information and ideas for trips, cooking, teaching, dancing, singing, and the list goes on and on. I have found that teachers who like to share with the colleagues inherently like to share with their students, which increases the knowledge and skill set of the students and translates into professional success for the teacher. The takeaway point here is that you have to get in the mindset of sharing if you want to be successful in education in China.

Summary

Being in a mindset of abundance is the key to being successful, not only in China but everywhere. When opportunities surround you, you will naturally become more positive, and your outlook will follow suit. When moving to a new country, one needs to have the ultimate mindset. This mindset involves having the foresight to prepare yourself to embrace future opportunities through:

- Appreciating the vast number of opportunities in China for the expat teacher,
- Learning the local language and culture,
- Understanding your own language and culture,
- Preparing your teaching and educational credentials beforehand,
- Getting teaching experience at home,
- Taking care of your health,
- Knowing yourself,
- Socializing,
- Don't take yourself too seriously, and
- Getting into the habit of sharing.

These guidelines will help you maximize your experience as an expat teacher in China and ensure that you avoid making the mistakes of those who came before you. Furthermore, these guidelines will allow you to become successful academically, socially, professionally, and even financially if you so desire. In the next chapters, I will outline the teaching environment in China and then proceed to present a step-by-step way for you to become a successful educator in China as you see it.

Part 1: Websites you Should Know About

Website	What you can do there	Link
Chinese Test	Learn about the HSK Chinese proficiency exam, get materials, and register to take the exam.	http://www.chinesetest.cn/index.do
Web MD – Fitness & Exercise	Medical advice and tips on exercising properly.	https://www.webmd.com/fitness-exercise/default.htm
Smart Shanghai	News in English related to life in Shanghai and also job opportunities.	https://www.smartshanghai.com/
Internations	An organized community for expats to meet online as well as offline.	https://www.internations.org
WeChat	China's number one chat and call app.	https://www.wechat.com/en

Part 1: Reflection Questions

1. What does it mean to have an abundance mindset?

2. Where do you see yourself in ten years? What will you have achieved?
3. What is your current fitness routine?
4. If you plan to go to China, what do you think your experiences will be like?
5. How much do you know about China, its culture, and history?
6. How many Chinese words or expressions do you know?
7. How often do you volunteer and support your community?
8. Why do you want to go overseas?

Part 1: Chinese Study Plan

Use this study plan to help you learn the Chinese language and culture. Remember, the journey of a thousand miles starts with a single step.

Monday	Tuesday	Wednesday	Thursday	Friday
Learn 5-8 new Chinese vocabulary words	Read or watch a television program or movie about China	Learn 5-8 new Chinese vocabulary words	Review the new vocabulary words that you have learned.	Practice speaking with a native speaker of Chinese

Part 2: Getting Ready

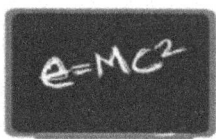

Now that you are aware of the situation in China and are in the process of developing the right mindset, you need to go out and get the right qualifications to secure your success. In this section, we will present the qualifications you need to secure employment, types of teaching opportunities, as well as how to apply for schools.

Qualifications Needed

To become a teacher at any reputable school in China, you need to have a bachelor's degree from an accredited school. This is a requirement for most jobs, not only in education but also for expats in China. I know of a former colleague who completed his bachelor's degree online at a school that was non-accredited in his home country. This was fine until the new policies in China emerged, which were more stringent in assessing the quality of foreign teacher's qualifications. As a result, the center was unable to sponsor his visa.

I will separate this next part into two sections. The first will be for those who are outside of China and planning to come here. The second section will be for those who are already in China.

1. **I am planning to go to China to be an educator.** - Make sure that your school has been accredited before you begin seeking employment in China. Also, your major is equally important. If you can get a degree from any Department of Education, that will be a benefit for up and coming educational professionals. The advantage of studying in the Department of Education is that many schools offer tracks for you to get your teaching license or certification as well. This effectively kills two birds with one stone regarding seeking employment in China. First, you achieve a bachelor's degree requirement for gaining employment. Secondly, you get your teaching license, which then gives you access to international and bilingual schools that offer top tier pay for expat educators in China.

If your goal is to become an educational leader, such as a school principal, then it will be better to major in Educational Leadership and Management through a Department of Education. This effectively gets you a third bird in that not only do you meet the bachelor's degree requirement, have access to the teaching license track, you also have a degree in leadership. This puts you in the top tier of top tier expats and opens doors for you to have leadership positions. Indeed, I most recently saw a post for a school principal at a famous international school where the starting salary was 1,000,000 CNY. Such a salary is more than enough to pay back any debt incurred on investing in a leadership degree. Of course, though, such positions generally require that the professional has had a certain amount of experience in leadership, which we will get to later.

Non-Department of Education Majors are also acceptable, especially if you majored in the humanities such as English, Mathematics, Psychology, etc. Some international schools offer teaching positions for these subjects. The downside, of course, is that you will need to go about pursuing your teaching certification on your own through external programs or, if you're lucky, through the international school. Some international schools offer the PGCE, which stands for Postgraduate Certificate in Education and is accepted as a teaching certification by many international schools. When interviewing with schools in China, it's best to ask if they offer a teaching certification track before accepting the offer if you do not already have your teaching certification.

You also need to obtain your federal or national background check. All foreigners seeking employment in China must have a clean, non-criminal background. Every country has different processes for how to obtain this, but generally, you will need to submit your fingerprints. At the current time, the background check should have been issued within twelve months of applying for your visa in China. So, make sure that your background check is up to date.

Finally, and most importantly, you need to have all of your degrees, teaching certification, and federal background check notarized by your country's government and authenticated by the Chinese embassy and consulate in your home country. There are several companies that you can pay who will do this for you. Still, if you want to save money, I recommend doing this yourself by simply contacting your school to have them notarize your degree and then going to the Chinese consulate or embassy yourself with your notarized documents and filling in the necessary paperwork. This final step is the most important as, without your notarized documents, you won't be able to get your visa sponsored. In addition, if you wait until you arrive in China to do this, you will either have to A) find a company to help you notarize all of your documents or B) go back to your home country yourself and do this.

2. **I Am Already in China. Is There Still Hope?** - The short answer is yes, but it's going to take some work. I wish I had had someone who would've told me to get my teaching license before I came to China. I had to complete my teaching license through an online program. Also, I had to pay a company to take my educational credentials, and non-criminal background check to be notarized and authenticated by the Chinese embassy in the United States. That aside, if you're in China at the moment, you are either on a tourist, spousal, business, or work visa most commonly. For those on a student visa, you'll need to have at least two years of work experience outside of China to make the following steps work for you.

No matter your situation, you'll need to get a bachelor's degree from your home country. If you're in China at the moment, you can complete your bachelor's degree online. Several accredited universities offer bachelor's degrees. You'll want to make sure that the program you choose is related to education, preferably through the Department of Education. However, as mentioned in previous sections, you can also major in English, Math, or any other subject if you're passionate, as international schools in China are keen to recruit subject teachers.

If the online Department of Education offers paths to teacher certification through their online program, that will be a plus and make your life easier. If not, I recommend using Teach Now (see link at the end of Part 2). Teach Now offers an online program that includes teaching practicums focused on the essentials of teaching. Upon completing the program, as well as passing the required exams, the student is conferred a teaching license by the District of Columbia in the United States. This is the path that I took while I was in China, and it worked well for me.

For those who want to pursue a career in management, there are many educational leadership programs from top tier institutions. I completed my online doctorate in Educational Leadership and Management at Drexel University. Since the program was offered as an online, hybrid, or offline course, the degree I received simply said Doctor of Education with no reference to the fact that the degree was completed online.

You will also need to get your background check completed. As you are already in China, you will usually need to get your fingerprints taken, and then you will have to send these overseas to be used by your government to process your background check. I will include a link in the description as to where you can get this done in Shanghai. For those in the United States, I will also include a link to an FBI channeling company where you will send your fingerprints. The channeling company will then forward your details to the FBI for processing. You will then receive your background check as a PDF online, which you can print out and submit for visa processing.

Finally, you will need to get your degree, teaching license, and background check notarized and authenticated by the Chinese embassy in your country. Your consulate may be able to notarize your degree, but you'll have to confirm this by yourself. In any case, there are three ways to do this successfully. The first way is that you can personally take these documents back to your home country and get them notarized and then authenticated. The second way is that you can mail the documents to friends and family back home and ask them to help you with the process. The final way is to ask a company to help you get the documents notarized and authenticated in your home country (link to one such company will be at the end of part 2).

As can be seen, it is possible to get qualified in China. Still, the process requires actively using online learning resources, reliance on external parties to assist with the notarization and authentication of your documents, and possibly higher expenses associated with getting the process completed. Nonetheless, if you're willing to put in the work to get the right job for you, it's possible whether you are outside of China or currently already in China. In the next section, we'll explore different types of teaching-related opportunities in China.

Types of Teaching-related Opportunities

In this section, we'll explore different types of teaching opportunities in China and how you can use each of these positions as steppingstones to develop yourself professionally as well as increase your income substantially. It's not necessarily the case that everyone who arrives in China will be qualified for high paying teaching jobs; however, that doesn't mean that one shouldn't make every effort to get the proper qualifications. It is also the case that, while making one's dreams come true, one needs to make money to pay the bills. As such, this chapter is split into two sections; first for people who haven't got the proper qualifications but working on getting them and second for those who have the proper qualifications.

1. **Jobs for Those Who Are Not Licensed Teachers But Considering Making Teaching A Professional Career In The Future** - If you're in China but currently do not have the necessary qualifications, here are some jobs that you can do in the field of education. Note that I am only listing the jobs that are related to education, as this experience can count toward your teaching experience when you later apply for teaching positions. Disclaimer: You should at least have a bachelor's degree before looking for employment. Also, if you don't have a bachelor's degree, then you're going to have to get one (an

online degree is the best option for those who are currently in China and underqualified). For those looking for employment as an English teacher, you need to have a bachelor's degree from an English-speaking country (e.g., the United States or the United Kingdom). As of right now, such positions below, except for the part-time and substitute teaching positions, may bring you a salary of around 15,000-20,000+ RMB/month.

A. Full-Time Jobs

    a. **Language Training Center Teacher -** Many expats who come to China get jobs as language training center teachers. Language training centers provide after school English lessons for children from the ages of three to eighteen years old. Other training centers offer language training for adults at a business or an independent center. Such jobs usually only require that you have a bachelor's degree. Schools range in size from very large institutions with tens of thousands of employees to small centers with five to ten employees. Centers, large or small, are ubiquitous in most major cities in China.

    The packages at large training centers might include a monthly salary and basic insurance. Teachers may or may not have paid holidays. In any case, normally, teachers work in the afternoons, evenings, and weekends. While this is a disadvantage for many, the advantage is that you can take your days off during the week or, if possible, take one day off on the weekend and one day off during the weekday. This means you can use the weekdays to get important things done at the bank or other institutions that might not provide the same or any services during the weekend.

If possible, I recommend getting a job with larger centers if you are just entering the world of training. The reason for this is that such institutions often pay for their teaching staff to be trained and, most importantly, certified to teach English to non-native speakers. While these certifications are not the same as the teaching license mentioned in earlier sections, certifications to teach English to non-native speakers will certainly be useful when teaching at international schools where a significant percentage of the students will be non-native speakers of English.

Finally, large training centers are also stable, for the most part, when paying teachers on time. The relative stability afforded by large training centers means that you can get the necessary support that you need to succeed in the world of language training if you are serious and passionate about it.

The downside of working in training centers is that such experience is rarely transferable outside of contexts where one is teaching English to speakers of other languages. Thus, for example, such experience gained might be more useful for moving to Japan, where non-native speakers similarly learn English as opposed to returning to the United Kingdom and teaching English literature. Next, it is difficult to be creative in terms of lesson planning and curriculum development. Training centers typically follow a set teaching regiment, and teachers are expected to follow. This is why I believe that small training centers are great places to work, as well. While they may vary in terms of efficiency and quality of the teaching materials, I do recommend that working for a training center, at least part-time, for the experience. In small training centers, the teacher likely receives feedback directly from the owner of the company. The teacher will possibly be in direct contact with the marketing person, the center manager, and director of studies, who will all communicate with others about business operations. This gives the teacher opportunities to interact with people whom he or she might not have access to in big companies. Furthermore, in small companies, everyone must wear many hats, so there will possibly be more opportunities to get experience in teaching, customer service, organizing events, managing people, and processes. The result is that you will have more experiences that will come in handy later when you decide to pursue leadership and management opportunities or decide to start your own business.

b. **Project Editor** - Textbook editors work for large training schools or publishers and create and edit content for learning materials. These jobs are your typical nine to five jobs, although it is common to work overtime when deadlines are approaching. The advantage of this job is that you usually will have the weekends off. In addition, for introverted people, this job is ideal as it primarily involves working in silence for the most part.

When I first came to China, I worked with a team of project editors who wrote language learning textbooks. The great thing about the experience was collaborating with different members of the product development team to create software and other support materials such as mp3 recordings. Another good thing was that there were opportunities to get promoted to more senior managerial roles within the product development team.

The disadvantage of being a textbook editor regarding teaching is that you won't be able to get any hands-on experience of actually teaching in the classroom. While creating textbooks will give you some familiarity with the learning process, nothing can even substitute getting real-life experience. Thus, if possible, should you become a project editor, you should request that your line manager allow you the opportunity of observing teachers use the materials that you have created.

c. **Publisher Promoter** - If you are more of the extroverted type, then the publisher promoter job is up your alley. Your employer will more than likely be a large publisher who sends you to various schools in the region to promote the company's latest teaching materials. This often requires that you organize a meeting with key individuals from a school such as a headmaster and other heads of department to introduce your company's teaching materials.

The advantage is that your company will usually provide training in terms of how to persuade schools to buy their materials. The company will also have professionals or specific guidelines for you to follow in terms of how to do demo lessons with potential clients. This will allow you to develop your interpersonal as well as teaching skills.

The disadvantage of being a publisher promotor is that your work schedule might not always be consistent. You may have to invite potential clients out for dinner, or you may have to visit their school early in the morning. In addition, this position, generally speaking, requires a lot of travel. You have to be comfortable traveling around the country.

d. **Local Stream Teacher** - The local stream teacher teaches a subject (e.g., most typically English) in a public school or in the local stream of an international school. Local stream simply refers to the fact that the majority or, in most cases, all of the students one teachers are Chinese citizens as opposed to international stream students where all of the students are foreign passport holders.

Oftentimes, you only need to have a bachelor's degree to get such positions when they are available. Generally speaking, you will need to work with a

Chinese homeroom teacher, and you will most likely share the classroom with multiple subject teachers. Class sizes can vary from relatively small sixteen to twenty at international schools to fifty or more in local schools.

The advantage of teaching in such positions is that this will allow you to gain some insight into Chinese culture and the art of teaching. The salary for such positions is usually sufficient to live as well as invest in your teaching certification. The disadvantage is that you won't have the same benefits or opportunities as a certified teacher.

This means that you will be limited in terms of what and how you can teach, which subsequently means your influence will not be as powerful. So, I recommend that you consider such opportunities for the duration of your contract with the intention of getting certified. This is not only going to bring you more success but is also going to help you develop the wealth that you need to have a better quality of life.

2. **Jobs For Those Who Are Licensed To Teach** - This next section is for those who have all of the necessary qualifications to become a teacher. In other words, the teacher has a teaching license, degree, and

background check, and all of these have been notarized and then authenticated by the Chinese embassy or consulate. Now, once you have this, you will be in a powerful position to take advantage of the higher-paying opportunities. Salaries can range from the 30,000 CNY/month to 50,000 + CNY/month in international schools in the tier 1 cities. These positions usually come with good family insurance packages, free tuition for up to two of your children as well as paid summer and winter holidays. Most importantly, the best schools offer professional development year-round. In this section, I am only going to write about the teaching and professional experiences that I have had or know enough about to be able to go into detail.

    a. **International School Teacher** - These positions are the holy grail of teaching opportunities in China. First of all, for those who are qualified, being able to get these jobs means that you can live in tier 1 cities and live a comparatively better life as a teacher than you could elsewhere (in the world I am willing to wager). The hours are typically between 8:00-4:00 p.m. Monday to Friday. There are a few professional development days on Saturdays, but these only take place about twice a year. Otherwise, your weekends are yours.

    The international school teacher may have his or her own classroom or may share a classroom with a co-teacher. The teacher is not only responsible for teaching subjects but also responsible for student well-being. In other words, your position might require you to be a homeroom teacher, where you can hone your management skills. In addition, you will be responsible for creating lesson plans and communicating with parents.

Your students will be foreign passport holders. Some of your students will be native speakers of English, some may be from countries with non-native speaking countries, and many may have a mom and dad who are Chinese citizens. Children whose mothers and fathers are Chinese citizens may have been born abroad in countries such as the United States or Australia. They have citizenship in those countries and thus are allowed to attend international schools in China. Note that most Chinese citizens are not allowed to enter the international stream at international schools.

Being an international school teacher puts you in contact with other teachers. Over the past ten years of being in China, I have met some of the most creative teachers who have a zeal and passion for teaching. They have influenced me greatly. Being around a team of passionate, qualified, and professional teachers can only make you better.

The disadvantage sometimes with working in the international stream is that you may sometimes find yourself inside of a bubble and not have access to the local culture in the same way that you would if you were teaching in the local stream. Thus, opportunities for learning the local language and culture will still be there, but such options will be fewer.

b. **Middle Manager** - Middle management positions are given to international school teachers who have demonstrated excellence in terms of teaching as well as professionalism when dealing with others. Such positions require one to lead and organize teachers to teach a particular subject such as English or Mathematics. Middle managers make slightly more than teachers, but the experience one gains from taking on leadership roles is a critical stepping stone to senior leadership and other opportunities. This is because, in addition to teaching knowledge, "people knowledge" is equally important. And the only way to get such knowledge is through the experience of working with, organizing, and developing teams.

Middle managers have a very challenging time as they have to deal with colleagues as well as senior management. In addition, they have to teach, as well. I thus highly recommend that teachers strive to get positions in middle leadership. This will give you the experience necessary to become wealthy and successful in China. You will understand why this is the case later in this book.

c. **Senior Leadership** -Senior leadership positions require that you have not only the proper qualifications but also experience in leadership and ideally have specialized in the role. These positions pay very well. I know of some positions advertising currently in Shanghai that pay up to 1,000,000 CNY/year and often include perks such as a driver. To secure such a position, you would have either been a school leader in your home country or have worked in middle management for some time. Each school has its own requirements for this position. My advice would be that a teacher demonstrates his or her loyalty to a school through dedicated teaching and leadership at the middle management level first, get qualified for the senior leadership role (see part 1), and then finally apply for this position.

The disadvantage of going after such a position is that it takes time, and there isn't a clear path to the position. It's a combination of factors that involves timing, experience, qualifications, and strong relationships with the school. However, if you are ambitious, I recommend that you at least try.

3. **Becoming Your Own Boss** - Becoming your own leader and starting your own business is possible for expats in China. There are companies (check the end of part 2 for links) that can help you register your own business. The costs for starting up depends on the business. It cost me about 5,000 CNY to get my study abroad consulting business registered through Shanghai Hengyu consulting company.

In the field of education, one type of business that expats can do is a study abroad consulting company where you help students study overseas. Another type of business might be a tourism company where you take people on study tours around the country. You might also consider starting a technology company where you create learning tools to sell to potential customers. No matter what business you do, you are responsible for following and obeying the laws of the People's Republic of China. So, if you decide to go the business route, I recommend that you consult with a local lawyer and find out what is possible and legal before you register a company.

The advantages of starting your own business are that you can sponsor your own visa, create invoices, and have the freedom to decide when and how hard you work. This is an amazing feeling that everyone should strive to experience, in my opinion. The disadvantages are that income may or may not be stable, and you have to provide yourself with benefits such as insurance. You also will probably have to work harder and longer than the average worker in the beginning until your business takes off.

I recommend that, in any case, you still get qualified, as mentioned throughout this book, before starting your own business. The reason for this is that customers or clients are more likely to support your business if you have the qualifications and experience to justify that support. In addition, having qualifications gives you options in case your business doesn't work out. You can be more confident in the process of setting up your business if you know that you can always fall back on your qualifications and credentials.

Doing business in China is always a matter of abundance. There are over 1.3 billion people, and thus if you are willing to go for it, you can find clients and customers. It is the ultimate test of confidence for one to start their own business. It is not for the faint of heart, but if you are determined or ambitious, you can make it work for you.

The following chart shows the advantages and disadvantages of the jobs listed in this section:

Position	Teaching License Necessary	Advantages	Disadvantages
Training center teacher	No	Teaching experience, Easy money	Weekend work, Odd hours

Project Editor	No	Experience learning about textbooks and materials	No teaching experience
Publisher Promotor	No	Experience learning about textbooks and materials, Sales experience	Working hours may change on a day to day basis, Limited teaching experience
Local stream teacher	No	Teaching experience, Can learn Chinese language and culture	Limitations in what and how you can teach
International School Teacher	Yes	Teaching experience, Higher salaries	Fewer opportunities to learn the local language and culture daily
Middle Manager	Yes	Leadership experience Stepping stone for senior roles	Must deal with multiple stakeholders and still teach
Senior Leadership	Yes	Leadership experience Privilege and perks	May take a long time to obtain

| Business Owner | No, but would be ideal if you are doing an education-related business | You are your own boss. Can potentially become wealthy | Risk of loss |

Avoid Making These Mistakes

Before we get into the art of teaching and making money, there are some common pitfalls that you need to avoid when you come over. The key thing is being able to make your money work for you. You cannot do this if you spend all of your money. Case in point, I recall a school principal who once asked me to help her transfer some money back home. Essentially, she asked me to transfer her entire savings. She had worked in the country for over a decade and yet only had a few hundred thousand yuan to show for it. She is not to blame. We have all made these mistakes. Fortunately, for you, you will know better than committing the mistakes below:

1. **Living in Overly Expensive Places** - This is a common problem. Expats often rent the most elaborately designed apartments with modern décor. Many don't realize that they can go for a cheaper apartment with the bare minimum of furniture and furnish and decorate the apartment with items from IKEA or things online from Taobao (the Chinese equivalent of Amazon) and achieve the same effect.

Others choose places where there are a lot of expat bars and restaurants. This isn't bad per se, but it can be a recipe for spending all of your hard-earned money in a heartbeat if you are not disciplined enough. I had an expat friend who recently borrowed money from me and still chooses to live in one of the more expensive places in Shanghai.

If you can, rent a place that's convenient but not too expensive. As a rule, the cost of rent shouldn't come to more than 20% of your monthly salary. In this way, you will have the disposable income to invest or save for a rainy day.

2. **Eating Out Every Day** - For many expats, eating out every day can lead to a dire situation. Bar bills can easily add up to thousands of yuan amongst friends. Steaks and hamburgers can also be expensive. While I am not saying avoid eating out altogether, I am saying that it is best to do so in moderation. Eating out 2-3 nights a week is ideal to ensure that you still have a social life.

Some days you can try to cook your favorite foods yourself by ordering the ingredients on Taobao. This past Thanksgiving, for example, I bought a whole turkey on Taobao for 200 yuan. I prepared stuffing, sweet potato pie, and vegetables at home by myself. The total amount spent on ingredients from Taobao came to about 650 yuan. The same meal in a restaurant would have cost over 1,000 yuan. Cooking at home can save you a lot of money.

3. **Not Negotiating for A Fairer Price** - Except supermarkets and large chain department stores, bargaining is common in China. When you go to the open market or visit street vendors, it's always wise to bargain and ask for a lower price. Most recently, I had an infotainment installed in my car. I was going to pay for it on Taobao for the cost of 1,800 plus free installation, which was already a deal. I decided to wait. Once I arrived at the shop, I asked the owner to lower the price. He suggested 1700, which was much lower than my expectation. I seized the opportunity and paid. Now, I have an infotainment system with GPS, forward and reversing cameras, Android apps, TV, and other apps for a price that I could live with. In China, bargaining is a way of life. Many expats pay the street vendor's initial price, offering only later to have realized that they could have saved by negotiation. If you feel uncomfortable asking for a specific lower price, you should ask if there are any deals. This is true when you eat at restaurants. Always ask if there is a combo or a special instead of merely ordering single items from the menu. This is going to save you a lot of money.

4. **Not Being Search Savvy** - Taobao is the app of choice when you're in China. You can get most of your daily necessities on Taobao, and these tend to be cheaper than the department stores and supermarkets. I can't tell you the number of times I went to purchase something outside only to return home and realize that I could have bought it for a significantly lower price on Taobao. In fact, in line with bargaining, you should always use the Taobao

price as a reference when bargaining with vendors. Except for some clothing items such as shoes or clothing that must be fitted, it is almost always advantageous to purchase items through Taobao. It saves time and will ensure that you don't get hot, sweaty, and frustrated running to and fro to find the things that you need.

5. **Not Investing Our Money** - There are multiple investment opportunities for expats in China. You can invest in real estate, the stock market, or bank investment options. Personally, I have invested in all three, but when I first arrived in China, I invested in bank options. The banks here have several investment opportunities that, at the time, had a 4-7% return on the initial investment. This was a great option for me at the time. For example, I invested 200,000 CNY, which gave me a return of around 10,000 at the time. During the period of investment at the bank, I wasn't allowed to touch the principal for about seven months. However, I was excited that at the end of the seven months, I had an extra 10,000 to spend. Effectively, my money was working for me. Instead of losing money, I was making money. I was able to acquire property in Shanghai using my savings. Since 2016 I have seen an exponential increase in my net worth in China as the property increased in value by 300% and is currently valued at over 1.4 million USD. It pays to have a rainy-day saving and doubly so to reinvest your money.

6. **Not Learning New Skills** - Having your degree and teaching credentials are just the start of your career

when you arrive in China. The next step is to learn new skills so that you can make practical use of your academic knowledge. Quick. Do you know how to make a high-quality YouTube video? Do you know how to use Adobe Photoshop? How about logotype? A lot of us have academic knowledge that gets forgotten as soon as we receive that paper called a degree. The supreme art of success requires that you take your knowledge and combine it with a skill to give in life in the real world. This is how you become successful and wealthy. The challenge is in learning skills, though, to turn your knowledge into a tangible expression for the world.

You need to learn skills from experts. While in China, you may or may not have access to those communities of people, but such a community does exist online. Skillshare is a wonderful app where you can learn a variety of skills ranging from photography to creative writing. Masterclass.com offers discussions, tips, tactics, and strategies in lessons that are given by the world's most successful people ranging from Chris Voss and Stephen Curry to Gordon Ramsay and Dr. Jane Goodall.

Summary

Continually improving and learning skills will help you in the classroom. As you learn new skills, you will find that you will develop newer insights into teaching as you utilize your skills to help students realize their potential. In addition, more skills lead to more success in terms of your career. It is my belief that the most enlightened and effective teacher is the teacher who constantly learns. It is equally important to learn from your mistakes and overcome them. In this chapter, we listed several mistakes most expats make after they move to China. I hope that you do not commit the same mistakes. I hope that you now have the knowledge necessary to get ready to embark on your journey to China to become an educational professional. In the next part of this book, we will explore methods of successful teaching in the classroom.

Part 2: Websites you Should Know About

Website	What you can do there	Link
International School Jobs	This is a database for international schools around the world. The system is designed for parents, but if you click on the link to the international school, you can easily find the jobs page and apply.	https://www.international-schools-database.com/
English First	Seek employment at English First training centers.	https://www.englishfirst.com/
Skillshare	Learn skills about business, animation, design writing, and more.	https://www.skillshare.com/
Masterclass	Skills, life stories, and strategies from classes taught by the world's elite.	https://www.masterclass.com/

How to invest in China stocks	Motley Fool article on how to invest in China.	https://www.fool.com/investing/how-to-invest-in-china-stocks.aspx
Bank of China Global Website	Find out about setting up a bank account as well as investment opportunities	https://www.boc.cn/en/

Part 2: Reflection Questions

1. What is your current level of experience in education?
2. What skills or education do you need to teach in the top tier international schools in China?
3. Have you lived overseas before? What lessons did you learn from the experience?
4. How much money would you like to make in China?
5. What do you estimate your budget for daily living expenses will be when you come to China?
6. What skills have you always wanted to learn but never had the time to?
7. What does it mean to make your money work for you?

Part 2: 6 Figure USD, 5 Year Wealth and Success Plan

Use this roadmap to help you get on your way to earning six figures a year.

	Year 1	Year 2	Year 3	Year 4	Year 5
Work	Training Center	School	School	School	School
Position	Teacher	Teacher	Middle Manager	Middle Manager	Senior Leader

Dr. William Clifton Green II

Study or Experience	Teaching License	Leader-ship	Leader-ship	Leader-ship	Leadership
Qualifications Needed	Bachelor's degree	Teaching License	Experience	Experience Network building	Experience Network building
Income (CNY)	20,000 /month	30,000 /month	30,000/ month	40,000-50,000/ month	60,000-80,000+ /month

Part 3: Success in the Classroom

Teaching in China is a wonderful opportunity to experience a new culture and society. It is important that we respect Chinese culture and customs and, at the same time, uphold the integrity of our own culture through our dedication to education. In this section, we will explore some key differences between Western and Chinese cultures.

In Chinese culture, teachers have a relatively high status compared to Western cultures, in my opinion. The teacher is considered the source of knowledge and the one who makes it possible for children to have opportunities to succeed in life. As such, most parents respect teachers highly and will follow the teachers' advice and opinions carefully. Thus, this next part is crucial for the educator who comes to China. Without a solid understanding of the situation, it will be difficult to become a successful educator.

In Chinese culture, academic performance is almost always given precedence over other areas, such as extracurricular activities. There are exceptions, but the norm is a preference for academics. Although this may seem like a blessing, it challenges the Western teacher for several reasons.

In Western culture, modern education aims to create a student-centered learning environment where the teacher is more like a guide than a commander. The idea is to develop students' abilities based on their individual needs and to differentiate the learning process to ensure that each student is making progress at his or her pace. For example, if I had a student who was struggling with math, and let's say, this student was a visual learner. I would assign activities for the child that would tap into his preferred learning style (e.g., graphics, visual stimuli) and also support his or her math skills. Furthermore, rather than drilling the student in completing math activities, I might encourage the student to engage in tasks such as interviewing students, making a survey, and tallying the results to determine if the child can use his or her math skills practically. In doing so, I could monitor this child's success and report to all key stakeholders (e.g., parents, the school leadership team, etc.) on the progress of this individual child. Such a teaching method can only ideally work if class sizes are small.

Traditionally and very common today in China is the practice of rote memorization and teaching. The idea here contrasts with the teaching style listed in the previous paragraph. In this style of teaching, the teacher is the center of the learning experience, the purveyor of knowledge, and the students are the recipients of this knowledge and experience. The advantage of this teaching style is that when there is a large number of students in a class, for example, fifty or more, the teacher can ensure that every child gets the same amount of information. Differentiated learning then is the responsibility of the training center or the parent. Traditionally, the teacher would have tutored children who needed support after class, but as far as I am aware, teachers are not allowed to this anymore.

Thus, for unfamiliar parents, when they observe a Western teacher teaching, it may be bewildering to them. First, Western teachers tend to have students get into groups and talk to each other. Whereas in the traditional Chinese classroom, students are not allowed to talk too much and rarely work in groups. Western teachers also tend to do less whole-class teaching. This leaves parents asking the question, "What did my child learn?" or they may say, "You need to give my child more attention." The assumption by many parents is how their child can "catch up" with everyone else as soon as possible. The idea here is that the majority of parents want their children to succeed academically, usually on tests, by outcompeting other students and becoming the top student.

Of course, not all parents feel this way, and there is a growing number of parents who think that the child's well-being is more important than getting top scores. Still, however, in my observation, the vast majority prefer academics and test success as the avenues for success are still primarily through academics. Thus, before I go into teaching tips and the art of teaching, there is some prep work that you must do with parents before you begin supporting their children.

First of all, if you are new to teaching, what you need to know is that academics around the world, including in China, realize that differentiated teaching and learning focused on developing individual student needs is better, in most instances, than whole-class teaching. Timely feedback and high expectations for all students are integral to good teaching. This information must be explained to parents at the start of the term. It's imperative to have a meeting with parents and present research, evidence, and clearly outline your teaching plans, priorities, and anticipated outcomes. In this way, you can ensure that parents are on the same page as you are, and when they come to observe your class (open days are very common), they will understand what you are doing. Before you set foot in the classroom, make sure that you've met with parents and explained the curriculum (what is to be taught) carefully and ask them if they have any questions. You might have a translator available who can assist with helping you find out the parents' concerns. In this way, you can mitigate some of the misunderstandings that may arise from cross-cultural differences involved in teacher delivery and feedback.

Overview to Success in Teaching

I will assume that you have already started your path toward teacher licensure in this section and will get to the root of what it means to be a successful teacher. If you haven't started down the path of teacher certification, then this section will help you to get in the right mindset. I tend to favor an eclectic approach to language teaching, learning, and syllabus design. In other words, there are many teaching strategies, approaches, and theories out there. I don't particularly care about any philosophy per se; instead, I believe that designing a syllabus should be, first and foremost, learner-centered. So the teaching method, strategy, and approach that you use, to my mind, must be made with consideration of the needs of the learner. How does one do this?

A good teacher is one who always conducts needs analyses before teaching. A well-designed needs analysis is imperative and a critical component of learner-centered classrooms. By needs analysis, we mean that teachers will take the opportunity to learn about their students (e.g., their hobbies, interest, learning strengths, and areas to support) through surveys, interviews, and conversations with students, parents, and all other vital members of the educational organization. Teachers should then use what they have learned to support student development. To be honest, having this understanding and executing in the interest of the student does not necessarily require teacher certification. For example, if the majority of the students in your class are kinesthetic learners and understand information by interacting with it, then it would naturally make sense to bring in 3D models when appropriate for children to see, touch, and learn from the interaction.

I also believe that learners must be provided with the opportunity to develop their autonomy. I must interact interdependently with teachers and fellow students to enjoy the benefits of a learner-centered syllabus. Autonomy in a classroom setting implies that the learner will take the initiative to gain insight into the process of acquiring knowledge or skill. I am convinced that taking the initiative is a prerequisite for controlling one's learning. When learners decide that they want to direct their own learning actively, they are, in effect, on the path to becoming more autonomous. Thus, the decision to become autonomous largely rests with our students and their views of language learning, learning in general, and how a classroom should be managed.

Ultimately, autonomy manifests itself when the learner takes steps to approach the target (which refers to whatever is being taught) through a variety of means, such as being able to incorporate knowledge and advice from peers and teachers in a meaningful way. To achieve this, students must believe that they have the abilities or skills to solve whatever problems they encounter. As a teacher, it's important to give students confidence, particularly in contexts where students may not have had the opportunity to express themselves in the classroom traditionally. The advantages of having an autonomous classroom are numerous.

Autonomous students also tend to reflect on processes that are conducive to autonomous learning actively. This naturally leads such students to contemplate and incorporate methods that enhance and expedite their progress. These students are also aware of their weaknesses and strengths to increase their performance in the subject being taught.

In addition, I believe that students must be taught to collaborate. All students, regardless of ability, must, at some point in time, work with others to ensure the welfare and success of everyone involved. When classrooms are structured to promote positive interdependence (i.e., engaging in meaningful actions that benefit everyone), our students will engage well with each other meaningfully and productively. This, in turn, will lead our students to gain more control over their learning to translate into learning success. We believe that interdependent classrooms provide for a more egalitarian classroom setting where students can participate confidently and openly with their peers without fear of rejection or being ostracized.

The development of student autonomy and interdependence corresponds with the creation of learner-centered curricula and syllabi, where learners take on a more central role in the learning process. Learner-centered curricula are based on the idea that adults learn best when they perceive new content as essential, contextualized, and relevant to their life experiences. In addition, students tend to learn better when they engage new information through a variety of different means (e.g., visually, logically, and spatially). As a result, teachers need to take into consideration the needs of the learner and place learners at the helm of classroom management. The role of the ideal expat teacher in China should be the role of a facilitator of the learning process. Do not tell the students the answer without first having let them have a go by themselves to try to figure it out.

At the same time, such a teacher should keep in mind that it is important to make learning relevant to students. In other words, the key question students always think as they sit in class is, "How is what I am learning useful for me in my current situation?" By the end of the lesson, the successful teacher would have provided the stimulus to support the answer to such a question. In doing so, the successful teacher gains the respect, admiration, and attention of the student who feels care for and supported.

One can think about it like this. Plants need water, but not all plants thrive in conditions where there is too much water, and many plants cannot thrive in places where there is too little water. If I give a cactus too much water, it will not thrive. If I forget to water my plants after a couple of weeks, I will need to buy more seeds! It is a similar thing when it comes to educating our children. There is no one size fits all. We have to think and think again to truly ensure that we are providing the best environment and support for our children. Finally, regarding the production, editing, correcting, and submission of written work, I believe that learners should have multiple opportunities to brainstorm, submit multiple drafts, engage in peer editing, as well as to consult with the teacher. Learners should maintain a diary or journal to reflect on their learning experiences as well as improve their writing in general. Reading for pleasure should likewise be encouraged, and print resources should be readily available in the classroom. This will be especially useful when teaching classes with students at varying levels and can be considered a form of differentiated teaching. The goal for the successful teacher is to provide a diverse array of learning resources, practice opportunities, and real-world applications to motivate and develop students' knowledge, collaborative and problem-solving skills, autonomy, and interdependence. Okay, now that the theoretical framework has been established, let's get into some practical stuff.

Putting Theory into Practice

These past ten years have been an extraordinary opportunity for us to learn connect with hundreds of students, parents, and teachers from all over the world. The challenges behind connecting such diverse people and cultures have been great indeed. However, through language teaching, my teams have managed to create a unique bond between people by helping students to communicate and express their ideas in various subjects. The ultimate goal then is to develop students who are multilingual, multicultural, and possess the values of integrity, honesty, respect, and compassion for others. When these students become adults, we believe that they will be able to create a better, more integrated world where all people have the chance to succeed if they so put their minds to it.

During these past ten years, we have taken our students on a journey. We have learned English through songs, dance, role plays, and movies. We have traveled to the China Art Museum and done research reports. We have performed on the stage, told jokes, studied hard, and completed quizzes. We have written poems, advertisements, as well as created posters and PowerPoint presentations. Amazingly, our students have done all of these things in a foreign language. As we move forward, it is necessary at times to reflect on the lessons of the past. In these lessons, as educators in China, we have learned something about ourselves and each other. As we keep score and look for ways to improve, these lessons serve as insight, a guiding light, that ever so subtly pushes us to the next level of performance. It is with this in mind that I share with you these lessons that I have learned as an educator:

1. **Student Interest and Motivation Come First -** Improvement cannot take place without the desire to achieve, and that is why students must be motivated to learn. Whenever you create a ppt or select materials for your class, you need to ask yourself, "Will, my students, appreciate this? Will this make my students excited to learn?" Student interest and motivation to learn should be the basis for decisions that you make.

2. **Teaching is an Art** - Only teaching from the textbook is not enough to help students achieve. A good teacher is one who can reach deep and bring out the best in his or her students. This requires many years of practice, a keen mind with excellent observation skills, and a genuine desire to want students to succeed. In other words, the content in the textbook is not as important as the content of the students' characters. Many boring teachers tend to overly focus on textbook content without striving for a balance between the theoretical and practical, the desire of the educational organization, and the desire of the individual students. Balance is evident in the best paintings. It is also ever-present in the best classrooms.

3. **Technology is Important** - Language learning can be enhanced by the use of technology in the classroom. Countless research studies support this. For example, some studies show us that students can get higher test scores when technology is used in the class to support their learning. My doctoral dissertation focused on using technology in the classroom to support student language learning. I found that students were able to improve the number of vocabulary words they learned in the classroom when they had the opportunity to collaborate while playing video games where they could learn new vocabulary words (see the link at the end of part 3 for the dissertation).

4. **Keeping Score is Important** - It's important to keep track of student performance, behavior and to chart

their progress as well as inform parents about what they can do to support student development. The successful teacher keeps detailed notes about his or her students. When asked about an individual student's progress, he or she has no problem speaking at length about the students' strengths, areas to improve, and the plan in place to support that students' development. The successful teacher displays student work progressively to demonstrate what the students have achieved and celebrates student success with appropriate feedback based on the evidence that he or she has collected.

5. **Students Need To Learn Twenty-First Century Skills** - Students need to learn how to collaborate, innovate, solve problems, be creative, use technology as well as communicate confidently to succeed in the future. Whenever possible, teachers should give students opportunities to collaborate and solve problems. What do I mean by twenty-first-century skills, though? As we all know, the work world is chaotic. Careers are no longer linear, and the guarantee of a job after graduating with a college degree is becoming less and less certain. One thing is certain; companies are looking for people with real-world skills. The problem, of course, is that schools often create students who are woefully unprepared to face reality and challenges of the real world. The skills needed to prepare for tests and negotiating a deal are vastly different. As educators, we have to prepare students to both succeed on tests (yes, they need to pass to graduate) and be successful in life.

And we need to let parents know that both skill sets are equally important in today's ever-complex world.

6. **We Are The Same** - No matter what culture we come from (Shanghai, Tokyo, Los Angeles, or London) or what language we speak, we are basically the same. We have the same hopes and aspirations, problems, and hardships. The more we learn about each other, the more our stereotypes are dispelled. It is the goal of the successful teacher to dispel stereotypes in the classroom. The successful teacher looks for and expands on commonalities that we share as a human species. He or she teaches students to be respectful, polite, and responsible global citizens.

7. **Everything is Love** - To achieve our goals, we need passion. Passion comes from being on one's purpose and devoting oneself to his or her unique cause. With passion, we can tap into a reservoir of limitless creativity and expression. It's important that we teach students to find their passion. The successful teacher asks students to reflect on their interests and then makes recommendations on how students can find their passions in life.

8. **Communication is Key** - Teachers and parents need to be in constant communication with one another to support student development. Strong leadership is necessary to connect everyone in the learning process to ensure the success of the center. That said, we cannot forget about our students. Their opinions matter as well. It's important that we listen to our

students and make improvements with their feedback too!

9. **Students Need to Move Around** - Sitting for hours in chairs isn't good for anyone. It's important to let our students move around, sing, dance, do some research, or simply reflect while standing. It is said that during ancient times, philosophers such as Plato and Socrates would have classes outside, walking around with their students, and reflecting on the world. Likewise, we believe that learning should target all the senses and cater to the multiple intelligences of our students. Some of the students are linguistics. Others are artistic. And yet others have spatial awareness, and a few are musical. We have to reach out to all of these students in the classroom using a variety of teaching methods and styles.

10. **Everyone Can Succeed** - We have had students from a cornucopia of differing backgrounds. No matter what their skill or level of learning, we have found that all students can be supported to achieve their learning goals. They only need the right kind of nurturing and guidance from teachers and parents to reach their desired destination. We need to put our biases aside and look at the bright side of each student and try to bring that out for the world to see.

11. **Be Positive About the Local Culture** - Try to learn from your co-teacher about how to communicate with your student's parents. Greet the parents when you see them and try to speak with them as best as

you can. Try to use some basic Chinese expressions to use during your daily life, such as when you go to the restaurant or meet friends. Take a weekend to engage in calligraphy and learn an appreciation for the local culture.

12. **Help Your Chinese Co-teacher -** If you have a Chinese co-teacher, you must work together with him or her. It is best if you are proactive in trying to make this partnership work. Try to get markers and resources from storage as well as set up the classroom and computers by yourself. Also, ask for lesson plans three days in advance to ensure that you receive them on time.

13. **Come Early to Prepare** - Showing up twenty minutes before class will ensure that you have enough time to prepare for the lesson. Always make it a habit of being punctual. Earlier is still better than later.

14. **Tidy up After Class** - Make sure all resources are returned, chairs folded, and desks placed correctly in the right location. Boards should be cleaned in preparation for the next class.

15. **Display Student Work** - Put student work up throughout the educational organization to help develop student confidence. When students take pride in their work, they are more likely to contribute more. The quality of their work will subsequently improve.

16. **Observe Other Teacher's Classes** - Learn from other teachers by observing their classes and gaining insight into how others teach. You will be amazed by what you can gain from observing other teachers' classes. Their techniques and strategies can help you to build up your teaching repertoire and maximize your effectiveness in the classroom.

17. **Connect with Your Students** - Remember, they may be young, but they're human too! It's important to connect with your students. Talk with them about their hobbies, interests, and day. Try to adjust and tailor your lessons to meet their hobbies and needs. Take a little time to communicate actively with your students as opposed to rushing to get through the curricula targets.

18. **Make Learning Fun** - You may be asking yourself what this has to do with communication. It has everything to do with communication! Making learning fun doesn't mean showing videos in the class or letting the children listen to the newest singers per se. Why do I say that? Because what is considered "fun" is really down to the students themselves. To find out what they like, you have to ask them! Don't be the teacher who decides what is fun or not without first consulting with the students first. Also, if you are unsure about what activities to do without consulting with the students, always ask the students to give their opinions after the lesson has finished. Teachers can determine the level of satisfaction of students by giving surveys.

19. **Give Students Personal Feedback** - Students should know their assessment results, their strengths as well as areas to improve, and how they can go about improving. Teachers need to be active in letting students know how they are progressing (not only during report card time) in terms of their academic performance as well as their life skill performance (e.g., collaboration skills, creative thinking, problem-solving, use of technology, etc.)

20. **Give Students a Voice** - Allow students to reflect on their performance openly as well as express their ideas and opinions during class time. Create a classroom environment where it is okay for students to communicate freely without fear of criticism. After all, developing students' confidence is essential if we are preparing students for the chaos of tomorrow. At least, they must have a solid personal foundation from which to derive inspiration, courage, and determination.

In Class Teaching Tips and Guidelines

Teaching for the past sixteen years has given me a lot of insight into how students think, develop, and succeed in their language learning. After you have started teaching at an educational institution, you will receive lesson plans and guidance to understand our teaching methods and structures. In this next section, I will provide advice in terms of best teaching practices to support you in developing the right mindset, attitude, and approach to teaching in the classroom. Here are some guidelines that all teachers should keep in mind:

1. **Follow The Lesson Plan** - When you receive or create a lesson plan, please make sure to follow the teaching plan, structure, and timing. While sometimes deviations can and should take place, the successful teacher can justify changes in planning and makes sure that his line managers are aware of the changes that are taking place as well as their justifications.

2. **Spend At Least 10-15 Minutes Before Class Reviewing The Lesson Plan** - It's important that you review the lesson plan, make notes about how you are going to proceed, think about how to support students who are at a lower ability and extend students who are at higher ability. That's right; teaching is not only about following the lesson plan because you need to consider those students who the lesson plan will not support. The lesson plan is written with the average student in mind. By average student, we mean the students who should be in the class you are teaching. In every class, you will find students who have lower abilities and students who have higher abilities. For these students, more is needed. For example, a lower ability student might need the teacher to give him or her more attention and support with vocabulary development. In contrast, a higher ability student in the same class might need encouragement to write longer sentences using connectives such as "because," "although," and "however." It's up to the teacher to know which students need support

and extension as well as how they plan to go about supporting and extending such students. Without a plan of support and extension, weaker students tend to drop out because the class is too difficult. Stronger students complain that the lesson is boring and uninteresting, and they subsequently lose interest as well. Thus, the good teacher is the one who can support all levels in his or her class by slightly modifying the content, focus, or approach to assist different levels to access the topic of discussion.

3. **The Big Four: Review, Quiz, Humor, And Games** - We were once all children, and we know how easy it is for children to forget what they have learned. Thus, it is essential for teachers to go back and review what they have taught and quiz students (not only written but verbally as well) to determine how well they have learned. In this way, the teacher can adjust his or her teaching style/practice to support students to achieve the desired outcome and also reflect on his/her teaching practice. Humor is also important. Connecting the learning to something interesting or exciting motivates students to learn and helps them better remember what they have studied. Also, humor can serve to help make a connection with the learning, thus increasing the possibility that students remember what has been taught. Finally, games are important. By games, we don't mean random games unrelated to the content. We mean educational games related to the key vocabulary, grammar, or topic of

discussion. At the end of every lesson, a quick game where students are given points for answering questions related to the topic of discussion can serve to motivate students to think about, reflect on and apply what they have learned in class. Best of all, such games tend to motivate students to persist in their learning regardless of their language level or ability.

4. **Communicate, Communicate, Communicate -** While it has been mentioned earlier in this book, it's worth mentioning it again here. Teachers need to talk with parents and students frequently about student progress **as well as what is being done (by the teacher) and what the parents and students can do to support student development**. The key thing is creating optimism by focusing on what can be done to improve the situation. Active communication ensures that parents and students understand that the center is serious about getting results and promoting our parent and student development.

5. **High Expectations for Student Success -** We never give up on children. No matter how naughty, every child can succeed. We often read about stories where students are belittled in school and grow up to become great people. Winston Churchill was such a student. His teachers wrote that he would never become anything; he was naughty and had no potential. Little did they know that he would become the leader of Great Britain during WWII and help

lead his nation to victory. As such, you never know who is sitting in those small chairs or desks in front of you. It might be a future world leader, speaker, doctor, politician, and the list go on and on! As such, as teachers, we have to hold all students accountable and believe they can succeed. Thus, we must ensure that students conduct themselves in a manner worthy of becoming great. They must sit properly, bring their resources to class, and complete homework on time. No exceptions. When it's time to participate, all students must take part in the class discussions. Parents and students must know that the teacher has high expectations for students to succeed.

6. **Managing Classroom Behavior** - Avoid shouting and screaming at students. Negative language should not be used when guiding students to behave properly. Instead, teachers should model positive behavior and communicate with parents about student behavior. In addition, putting students in timeout is against the law in this country and making students stand up or go out of the classroom for misbehavior is culturally inappropriate. It goes without mentioning that we should all take student safety seriously.

Office Communication

When you start at you're your educational center, many of the key interactions that take place daily happen in the office space. Senior leaders and middle managers often have meetings with staff in the office. Subject teams also have group meetings in the office. Finally, parents and students come to the office for meetings and feedback. It's important to make this space into a positive environment that promotes positive communication. Flowers, bright colors, positive quotes, and artwork are essential elements to making this space conducive to proactive cooperation. In addition, here are some rules for interacting with the various stakeholders who come into the office space:

1. **Interacting with Colleagues**

    A) **Integrity** - This means doing what we say we are going to do. For example, if you say that you can finish a lesson plan by a particular time, you make sure to do so and to hand it in on time. Keeping your integrity is the key to building a positive, enduring reputation. The successful teacher is mindful of coming on time, of not over committing and not make promises unless he or she is sure that it can happen.

    B) **Cross-Cultural Competence** - This means understanding Eastern and Western Cultures and how to communicate with colleagues from these two different backgrounds. For example, some topics about politics or race may be considered taboo or inappropriate in some cultural contexts. The best thing to do, in any circumstance, is to have an open mind and ask questions when you're not sure. You also need to be willing to compromise and make changes where necessary.

C) **Respect** - Always be polite and courteous. Expat and local staff should greet one another, and staff should greet everyone when they enter the office. Members of the staff should address each other by their given names. Staff members should model polite language such as "please" and "thank you" for the students and should endeavor to use such language in the office space. When staff members make mistakes, line managers should be firm but polite when giving feedback. The goal is to create a comfortable space for those who are trying their best while at the same time ensuring that all members of staff respect the organization and are striving to uphold the values of my English.

D) **Active and Timely Communication** - Notices of sick leave should be given in and line managers informed in line with the company's policy. Local and expat teachers should be proactive in their communication. For example, if someone hasn't received a lesson plan, rather than waiting the day of the lesson to inquire about lesson plans, do so two days in advance to avoid not having an adequate amount of time to prepare. Expat and local teachers should inform each other of what was covered and taught in the lesson so that co-teachers can plan and prep for the following lesson. All staff should report when anything is broken, not working properly or when anything is present in the workspace that may cause danger or be a disruption. An important rule of thumb here is always to try to communicate as early as possible to avoid conflict.

E) **Leadership Communicating with Team** - Some readers of this book are going to take on leadership roles in China. Here is some advice about how you can best communicate with the team:

- **Maintain Positive Relationships:** For all leaders, it's important to maintain essential to maintain a positive relationship with all staff and keep the morale of the team-high.

- Schedule Brief Meetings: Schedule brief five-minute one-to-one meetings with staff. You should find out their work-related needs. The goal is to listen without judging. Try to do this monthly.

- **Communicate Openly:** Encourage the staff to talk with each other, communicate openly, and share ideas in the office space. If the workspace is not open and people are not talking, try to encourage them positively by starting a conversation. Humor is appropriate in these situations as well. Say thank you to the staff often and encourage everyone to be positive.

- **Support and Protect Staff:** Leaders should always respond positively on behalf of teachers and work as a mediator between the school, staff, and parents.

- **Share Teaching Ideas/Resources with Staff**: Use the school website and share timely updates and resources with staff.
- **Send Timely Reminders and Updates**: Send school holiday schedule updates via WeChat (for example, October holiday updates, etc.), so the staff is aware of when they need to come to work or when there are changes in the schedule.

2. **Avoiding Open Conflict in the Office Space** - Sometimes, conflict is unavoidable. While this is understandable, open conflict in the office space is, more often than not, strictly prohibited. If disagreements occur, both parties should seek to remove themselves from the office space. For example, going to a café to discuss issues can be productive. Sometimes waiting a while before engaging when disagreements occur can help to allow both parties to come up with a feasible solution that works for both sides. Keep in mind that you are a representative of your educational institution. Loud disagreements, arguing, fighting, or shouting are detrimental to the company image and reputation.

Communicating with Parents

The parents, at any of the educational institutions, are the most important client and stakeholder. They make decisions about whether their children will enroll at the institution or not. As such, all members of staff must keep in mind that respect for parents is fundamental and paramount to the success of the institution. The following guidelines will familiarize you with how you can provide quality service to parents.

A) **Greeting Parents -** When parents are in the office, near or inside of the classrooms, staff are expected to smile and greet the parent. For expat teachers, saying "Hello" or "How are you?" is sufficient even if the parent cannot respond.

B) **Quality Customer Service** - Particularly, when new or potential parents are in the office, staff must follow these guidelines:
   a. If the parent is standing up or looking around in a confused manner, show them where to sit and offer them tea or water. If a child is with them, offer the child some water.

   b. Find out why the parent has come to the center. Write down their contact details and refer them to the relevant person who can help them. Never keep parents waiting long. Try to help or support as quickly as possible!

C) **Communicate Actively About Student Performance** - Parents should be kept frequently up to date about their students' performance in class. However, giving feedback isn't enough to help students succeed. Teachers also need to inform parents:

   a. **How the teacher and school will support the individual child to succeed.** This means that the teacher needs to think about differentiated instruction and how the child's strengths can be utilized to help him/her improve.

    b. **How the parent can support the child at home.** The parent needs to be informed about what he/she can do to support their child at home. The combination of in class/at home support needs to make sense for the parent to understand how the teacher's learning plan is going to help the child succeed.

D) **Use the Sandwich Approach when Giving Feedback** - When giving feedback to a child, do not give overly positive or negative feedback. Instead, use the sandwich approach. Start with something positive about the child's performance (and or character), then tell the parent some area where the child could improve. Finally, conclude the conversation with something positive or encouraging about the student, the student's expected performance, or any future support that might be beneficial for the student. The sandwich approach is a positive way to give feedback and will ensure that the school and parent are focusing on student improvement.

E) **Act on Parent Feedback:** When a teacher receives feedback from the parent, he or she should reflect on it and not be quick to dismiss it. Suggestions from parents should always be brought up in the weekly staff meetings, and when parents give feedback (whether useful or not), teachers should politely thank parents for their feedback.

Communicating with Students - Students are the most important stakeholder within the organization. Without students, there would be no school. Students are critical in determining whether the content/structure/teaching style of the lesson is interesting, motivating, and worthwhile, as well as whether the teacher in question is suitable for them. These decisions ultimately determine whether parents want to continue studying at an institution or move elsewhere. As such, student motivation and interest to study are high on the priority list for every teacher.

Avoid shouting and screaming at students. Negative language should not be used when guiding students to behave appropriately. Instead, teachers should model positive behavior and communicate with parents about student behavior. In addition, putting students in timeout is culturally inappropriate, as is making students stand up or go out of the classroom for misbehavior.

When it comes to communicating with students, understand that in my experience, children follow an adult's actions rather than their words. So, if you want students to behave and improve, you need to model it. For example, if you want students to sit correctly, show them how to sit properly, and make sure that you sit properly when you sit. If you want students to be polite and courteous, you need to be that way when you communicate with them. If you want students to improve, you need to give timely feedback on the steps they need to take to improve. The successful teacher in China is the one who best uses feedback to prepare students for success academically in the short term and professionally in the long term.

Summary

This chapter explored the art of teaching and how to achieve success inside as well as outside of the classroom. The key to helping students become successful is for the teacher to realize that he or she is not only assisting students in mastering academic content but also helping them to succeed in life. As such, the teacher needs to prepare lessons that focus on developing the whole child through a variety of differing stimuli. Students need to have the opportunity to collaborate, problem-solve, innovate, and think independently. As the student makes progress, it is up to the teacher to give timely feedback to parents and students, communicate effectively with all stakeholders, and guide the student in the direction of success.

Part 3: Websites you Should Know About

Website	What you can do there	Link
Howard Gardner	Learn about Howard Gardner's theory of Multiple Intelligences and how it relates to student learning.	https://howardgardner.com/multiple-intelligences/
My dissertation	Learn about how technology supports Chinese students' English language	http://tinyurl.com/wsn38hf

	development in the classroom.	
Edutopia	Learn about six ways to promote student autonomy.	https://www.edutopia.org/article/6-strategies-promoting-student-autonomy
Scholastic	Learn about differentiated instruction.	https://www.scholastic.com/teachers/articles/teaching-content/what-differentiated-instruction/
Weareteachers	Learn about classroom management	https://www.weareteachers.com/what-is-classroom-management/

Part 3: Reflection Questions

1. What does a learner-centered education mean to you?
2. Think about your experiences as a student. Who were the teachers who inspired you? How did they do that?
3. Why is it better to praise positive behavior than punish negative behavior?
4. What does it mean to be firm but fair when it comes to classroom management?
5. How can you create a positive office space?

Part 3 Assignments

These are assignments that I gave my teachers in the past in regard to thinking about best practices when it comes to classroom management and teaching. I encourage everyone to try these activities to reflect on what was discussed in this part of the book.

Assignment 1: Developing the Whole Child - In education, there has been a movement in recent times that focuses on developing the whole child. Or, in other words, developing a child's skills to be successful in life through utilizing his or her strengths and improving in areas that may hinder his or her success. How do you envision developing the whole child as a teacher? Write a one-page reflection.

Assignment 2: Technology in the Classroom - Task: Do some research on educational software that can be used in the classroom. You can A) watch a video of the software being used or B) if you are a teacher, get the permission of your school first, and then use the software in your class.

Tips for Using Technology in the Classroom

- Try to use technology in the class to increase the interest of the students.
- Make sure the content is related to what is being taught or studied.
- Make sure students know the rules about how to use technology effectively, how to work with others, and behave safely.
- Use in moderation (5-10 minutes should be enough).
- Assess children's understanding of the gaming/video content after the activity has finished.

Reflection Questions

- What did the children learn?

- What did the children think of the activity?
- Was it effective? Why or why not?
- What would you do differently next time?

Part 4: How to Make a Passive Income in Education

In this section, I will cover how to make passive income as an educator. Passive income refers to income that you make when you are not working. The amount of money a person can make depends on their effort and ability. There is a correlation between the amount of money a person makes and his or her ability to form positive relationships with others. Normally, a person can develop good relationships with others when he or she is passionate. This is because such a person can inspire others with his or her experience. If you've read this far in the book, you know what it takes to inspire people in education.

I can assure you that by following the strategies listed in this book, you can come to inspire your students, your line managers, and the parents of the students you teach in China. Subsequently, when you do this, you will become very successful in the field of education. However, I need to stress here that success is a mindset and exists in this form before it translates into financial success. As mentioned earlier in this book, you must have the mindset first before you can make a profit. The bigger your mindset, the more you will gain. If you were to ask me what the mindset is, all I can say is that it is not about profit. Instead, it is putting others first. It is a love of helping others -- teachers, students, your leaders, and your community. This is the mindset. If you are in this for profit solely, you will never make it. If you are in it strictly for yourself, you will find support long and coming.

In this next section, I will tell you how you can support others and make a profit. Let me warn you, though, that if you are not in the education business to support others, then you will not have the necessary energy to persist or the will not to quit when things are hard. If you have read about what it takes to be a good teacher, then you know consideration for the student is key to success as a teacher. If we take this same logic to the next level, you will realize that consideration for the team is the key to success as a manager, and consideration for the school is the key to success for the school principal. Then to be successful when it comes to making money is to have consideration for those who give you money (i.e., the customers). It sounds simple, but the truth is that most people cannot truly understand what it means to dedicate their lives in service of others.

The idea of service has a negative connotation. This year, I made 2,000 CNY selling my used clothing on an app in China during the pandemic. It was an experiment that I planned. I wanted to see how fast I could sell some used things of mine. Eventually, I found a buyer and took all my clothes to the street to sell to others. People were watching me curiously as I made the transaction. They asked me how a guy with a PhD could (well, technically EdD) do that. "You're a doctor with a PhD," they said. I guess that means that I should be proud. I shouldn't talk to anyone or sell anything. In that case, I wouldn't help anyone. My question to those people is, "How much is pride worth?" Nothing.

I know many PhDs in Shanghai. One guy, in particular, was a potential partner. We were trying to negotiate a deal with him. He insisted that he receive over 50% of the profit, although all he had was knowledge. He refused to negotiate and proceeded to get aggressive. Another partner who was actually in charge of bringing the students was worth more than that guy, but she only asked for 30%. Long story short. I saw him one day when I was driving home. He was walking on the street looking angry as if the world owed him something. He had to leave due to a lack of opportunities, eventually. If only pride were worth something, he would be worth a million or more. Instead, he ended up frustrated without much. The other partner is now heading the program and making more profit than what she initially asked.

I know another local woman; she doesn't have a PhD. She's wealthy and has several businesses. Her newest venture is selling discount restaurant tickets on WeChat. She's shared her events with everyone, including me. She made it so that I could treat my loved ones to a Japanese dinner worth over 1000 CNY, and I only paid 200 CNY. She helps people for a living and has a son and a daughter who are both enrolled in international schools. She is making a lot of money in her main businesses, but she is not afraid to try new things such as selling discount restaurant tickets. Most people would say that it is beneath her, but she's humble and willing to sacrifice face for an opportunity. She's successful. The guy with the PhD is depressed. Not that I have anything against people with PhDs. I am simply highlighting that this is the difference between those who make it in life and those who don't.

Ego and pride are far away from those who find financial success through honest means. To be rewarded for your efforts, you have to have the mindset that you are doing what you're doing for the sake of others. And sometimes you're going to have to get way out of your comfort zone. There were times when I stood out on the street, passing out fliers for my business. We wanted to help people, and that's why we were there. We didn't care what people thought about us. The joy of trying a new venture and of experimenting with the unknown is what gave me the drive to be persistent. This joy can motivate you, as well. The secret, though, is that you have to stay humble and be willing to learn. You also have to understand that as you get more and more qualified that you will find that the challenges will be greater and greater. The level of experimentation and knowledge required to address these challenges will require that you work and interact with many people. You have to win their hearts through your humility as well as your desire to ensure and encourage success and promote high expectations.

I've primarily made money through copyright, businesses, online courses, the stock market, and property investments in China. These investments were made with money gained from teaching initially, and then the investments themselves made money passively. You have to start small to make it big, and you're going to have to budget how much you spend so that you can have extra money to invest. You have to hold yourself accountable to keep your budget as well as have the discipline to put in the time and effort to make everything work.

I will go through each of my investment strategies below detailing what I did. When it comes to investing your money, you should take the time to do the research to see if the opportunities are worth investing in. Also, at the end of Part 4, I will introduce two websites where you can begin making money as soon as you enter the education industry using the skills you already have. If you remember nothing else as we progress through this section, remember that knowledge is power. You can gain knowledge best through trial and error, as well as socializing with others. At the heart of this drive for success is a mindset of humbleness and a willingness to grow and learn. In theory, teachers should understand this mindset better than most because it is the mindset of a successful learner.

How to Profit in The Field of Education

I am going only to list a few examples below, as I think these examples will give you an understanding of the bigger picture in terms of how I generate income.

1. **Doing Business** - I also did several educational related businesses, specifically regarding helping students prepare to study overseas during various periods between 2010-2020. I organized several VIP services aimed at preparing students to enter Western institutions. Parents asked for services such as helping them to understand Western culture, preparing them to study in academically rigorous environments as well as tips on how to succeed in Ivy League schools. My support was well sought after because these students almost always succeeded in international learning environments. Each

parent paid me around 20,000 CNY/year per child and 1,000 CNY an hour for a private one-to-one consultation. During the past decade, I've helped hundreds of students.

The key to success lies in offering high-level training. At the time, there were a lot of "backpacker teachers" or people without qualifications working as teachers in the EFL (English as a Foreign Language) market. I once observed one such teacher. She observed the students tease one another for one hour and then seemed puzzled when I asked her what the focus of the lesson was.
Contrastingly, when parents came to us, we offered them value for their money by accurately assessing student needs and providing quality student-centered instruction. Subsequently, our students made rapid progress, and parents started recommending our centers via word of mouth. This is what led us from having eight students to over five hundred. We did very little, if any, advertising. I wholeheartedly believe that a good product or service speaks for itself. The important thing is that no matter what you do, you've got to get results first. The money will come later.

Doing business is relatively straightforward in China. You'll need to register your business and get all the proper certifications. There are companies, such as Shanghai Hengyu Consulting company, which can support you with getting certified. They will also help you get your company chops, register your business bank account, set up your company invoicing as well as apply for you to sponsor expat visas in China. Companies such as Shanghai Hengyu make the process easy.

While going through the process of setting up your business, you're going to need to consult with a lawyer. Many lawyers, especially in the bigger international cities of Shanghai and Beijing, speak English. If you don't reside in these cities, it may be worth taking a trip to consult and add a lawyer via WeChat. The connection will be meaningful as you navigate the business world in China. I make sure to message my lawyer before engaging in any business deal.

Next, if you're just beginning and have set up your company, you need to get out and meet people. Business is not going to come to you. No one is going to come and knock on your door and put money in your hand. You're going to have to meet people. The current app of choice for meeting in China is Internations (see the key links in part 1). There, you will be able to connect with professionals and find potential partners to work with or, in some cases, individuals who can introduce you to clients and customers.

Joining WeChat groups is another way to meet people. I am a member of at least a hundred groups ranging from topics such as "Blood Type O" to "Electronics" and "Expat Support" groups. Whenever I want to promote my business, look for potential employees, or ask a question, I post in these groups. I've also created my own groups of people who I've added to my network. My lawyers, employees, friends, and connections can all be found in one such group. WeChat groups make life easier when it comes to doing business.

2. **Copyright Ownership** - In 2018, I created a curriculum for an early education course for students aged three to five years old. Materials and assessments were also created for this course. Then, I was approached by an organization that was familiar with the courses that I have designed in the past. For the courses that I create, I always apply for the copyright. When an organization contacts me, they can use the course, but they have to pay me a percentage of their revenue based on the number of sales they get. I spent around 5,000 CNY on legal fees to get the copyright last year. So far, the current agreement with the organization using my course brings me about 5,000 CNY a month and is increasing as the number of students in that organization increases. I anticipate it will triple by the end of the year.

Getting a copyright is relatively straightforward if you have a lawyer. The lawyer will help you with registration. What you need to do, though, is keep track of the courses that you have designed. If you're completing a teaching program, there may be a class or two where you will need to create a syllabus or curriculum. Take these classes seriously. You may just be developing an idea that you can get a copyright for. Business owners from outside the field of education are willing to pay a premium for ideas. In recent years, many people in China are eager to get into the billion-dollar education business but have no idea where to start. They have the capital, and you have the know-how. It's a win-win situation as long as you have a lawyer who can help you negotiate a good deal. With your ideas, they might be able to build a multi-million-dollar business. If you possess the copyright to those ideas, you will also be able to profit hugely when their business develops.

3. **Online Courses** - I have also created online classes using Udemy. Udemy is an asynchronous online learning platform that I will introduce later in this book. I highly recommend it. I created all the content for the coursework a couple of years ago. One course I created for this platform was on learning English in preparation for the IELTS exam. The other course is about how to lose weight and get in shape. Hundreds of students have signed up for these courses, and I still receive passive income every time someone signs up. After a little hard work and effort, you can reap the benefits for years to come using Udemy.

I think making passive income online is becoming easier and easier. Everyone knows a few platforms to go to consume content and watch movies and listen to songs, but few people think about how to use those platforms to earn a passive income. As an educator, I can recommend two platforms where you can start generating revenue using the skill set that you are developing. This is income that you can save or reinvest into more significant projects that align with your dream and vision. Now, let's focus on two ways you can make money while you are completing your teaching certification and/or teaching.

1. **Teachers Pay Teachers-**

   (https://www.teacherspayteachers.com/) - Teachers pay Teachers is a website where you can upload educational materials that you created (ppts, flashcards, handouts, classroom banners, how-to videos, podcasts, etc.) and sell them to other teachers for money. Of course, that said, you should only upload materials that you have created yourself. Never upload the materials of others or your school without express permission.

I think this is a great website as when you are completing a teaching licensing program, and you will be asked to create learning materials. You could then turn these assignments into products that you can sell to other people who might find them useful. This can be a win-win situation where you gain knowledge about the profession and also earn a passive income. This is because once you've uploaded your materials, you can continually generate income years down the road.

The more materials you upload, potentially, the more money you can make. If you become good at doing this, you can generate most of your income through the platform. This will require persistence and carefully taking on feedback from the customers who purchase your product. Remember, you need to put the customer first to succeed.

2. **Udemy** (https://www.udemy.com/) - Udemy is a wonderful online platform where people create online courses. The courses are asynchronous. In other words, the classes do not happen in real-time. Teachers upload videos create quizzes, and other activities. Then they activate the course, and students enter. Teachers can decide how long they want their class to be and how much they want to charge for their courses. You can

create as many courses as you like. You can also create coupons and discounts for your courses.

The good thing about Udemy is that you can create courses about any topic. For example, if you want to create a course on how to play the guitar, you can. Likewise, if you want to create a course about statistics, you can do that too. This gives you flexibility in terms of what you can teach. You don't need a teaching certification to use this platform so that you can start your courses at any time.

The advantage of having a teaching certification is that it will better help you understand the learning process, which ideally should support you in developing higher quality courses. The user interface for developing courses on Udemy is straightforward and relatively easy to learn. Once you've created your first course, creating the next course will be a breeze. As with Teachers Pay Teachers, the more courses you create on Udemy, the more money you can potentially make.

When it comes to getting people enrolled in your courses or purchasing your content, you can rely on the platform itself to bring your customers. After all, people go to these platforms searching for materials. Additionally, you can promote your work yourself. One way to promote your work is to set up a channel on social media promoting your courses and content. The other way is to inform relevant people in the academic community about your courses and content. In doing so, you create multiple opportunities for people to know about the work you are doing and how you can support them. The bigger your social network, the more you will be able to get the word out about what you are working on. This can translate into more opportunities for you to make money.

Respect your School and Respect the Law

Finally, regarding making money in education, I think everyone should be excited about the opportunities that await in China. I recommend that once you arrive, you get a lawyer who you can consult with about what is legal and what is not concerning doing business. In addition, a lawyer can assist you with getting copyrights for your creative work.

You need to do your homework to determine what is possible in the business climate. Doing the research about the laws of China will help you to make better decisions about how to move your business forward in the right way. A lot of what you can do will depend on whether you are doing your own business or working for others. For example, if you are working for a school, you need to follow the contract carefully. Many school contracts have specific statements or requirements concerning part-time work. Respect the school that has given you opportunities. Your contract will say what you can and cannot do regarding additional part-time work. Whenever in doubt, consult with your line manager and HR and always consult with your lawyer.

Where Do I Go from Here?

Actually, if you notice, the majority of this book was spent on talking about how to get qualified and the art of teaching. This is because the hard part is actually in getting qualified and understanding how to be an effective educator. Without the fundamentals and the right growth mindset, it will be difficult to become financially well off in this land of abundance. However, once you have the qualifications and experience, it is easy to make money provided you have established a positive reputation. And yes, people talk, so you have to put your passion into every lesson and try to be cordial when dealing with everyone. Once your reputation is established, people will come to seek you out, provided that you are a good, down-to-earth person who is charismatic and easy to communicate with.

Of course, you need to decide how you want to make money in China. Do you want to work for a salary, do your own business or earn passive income from online courses, copyright, or other types of investments? So, the first step to accumulating wealth is to decide how you want to proceed. Make a detailed plan about where you see yourself in five years. It seems fantastical, but it is necessary, and it works. Trust me. Let me share with you a letter that I wrote in 2005 detailing my plan to a friend (there are some Japanese words in the letter as I wrote this letter to a friend who I met in Japan).

The Art of Becoming a Successful & Wealthy Educator in China for Expats

William Green <williamgreenii@gmail.com>   Mon, Aug 1, 2005, 7:15 AM
to X

Dong,

What's up man? How is it going?

I am working at an English school in Aichi (in the inaka man!). I decided not to go to China now, but I will be going there in about a years time to begin doing business in the middle country. So I have been studying Chinese seriously these days and doing a great deal of research. I am interested in starting an English school there and also investing in some real estate. Of course, I will need a great deal of capital in order to make the latter a realization. I am also trying to determine which region/province will be the best to invest in.

I am studying to take the 2 kyu Japanese language proficiency test in December as well. xuexi, xuexi, zai xuexi.

Please take it easy in all of the humid weather.

dewa mata renraku shite naa!

Billy

At the time, I had just graduated from the University of North Carolina at Chapel Hill. I had only been to China once and had no idea about what it would take to make this dream happen. I wrote it down, and it came into existence five years later. Perhaps, I was having a conversation with my future self, and this revelation revealed itself. Or maybe, I simply created a positive self-fulfilling prophecy that was embedded in my subconscious. This belief somehow directed me toward the goal of coming to China. No matter the reason, it's important that you write down a plan and speak your future into existence. The universe will then do its part to make sure it happens as you envisioned it.

Finally, after you have made it, you need to share your experiences with others. You can write books, as I have. Or you can create videos online detailing your experiences. Sharing with others is one of the keys to success in the business world. The more you help others with your talent or passion, the more successful you will be. In China, there are 1.3 billion people who are waiting for you to share your talent and passion with them.

Summary

To generate wealth, you're going to have to start with a plan. You need to decide exactly how you want to make money, as well as your vision for success. Do you want to be a school principal or classroom teacher? Do you want to start your own business, or do you want to work for others? Do you want to create passive income online? You need to ask yourself these questions before beginning your quest to China.

In addition, don't only talk about where you see yourself in five years; write it down. Share your plan with close, supportive friends. If you decide to come to China and are getting certified as a teacher, set up accounts on Teachers Pay Teachers and Udemy. You can start creating learning and course content on these websites that can generate passive income for you while you work on getting qualified and establishing your career. Remember, you need to start putting people first to be successful. Think about how you can contribute to the world to make it better. When you take this approach, you will find that mindset will be wealthy, and subsequently, your income will follow suit.

Let me conclude here by saying that everything takes time. It may be five years before your dream gets off of the ground or longer. You've got to be prepared to be in the field for the long haul if you want to be successful. Anyone who claims to have a fast track method is a charlatan. It does take hard work. But hopefully, after reading this book, you will have a clearer understanding of what it takes to be a successful educator in China. You can do it if you believe you can and stick to your vision and plan.

Part 4: Websites you Should Know About

Website	What you can do there	Link
Udemy	Create online courses and make money.	https://www.udemy.com/
Teachers Pay Teachers	Create learning content and make money.	https://www.teacherspayteachers.com/
Summary of the 48 Laws of Power	Summary of the 48 Laws of Power by Robert Greene. Learn about power and success.	https://alldayprogress.com/48-laws-power-list-summary
Joint-Win Law Firm	I have hired lawyers from this firm in the past. Consult with these lawyers.	http://shanghai.lps-china.com/partners/shanghai-joint-win-law-firm/

Part 4: Reflection Questions

1. What's your vision and dream?
2. Set a realistic date when you think this vision and dream will come to fruition. When is it?
3. Where do you see yourself in five years?
4. Are you prepared to sacrifice to make your vision and dream come true?
5. How much active income do you want to make?
6. How much passive income do you want to make? How will you do it?
7. What do you intend to do with your income?

Part 4: Passive Income Plan

Month 1: Study

Step 1: Set up an Udemy account. Study the platform.
Step 2: Set up a Teachers Pay Teachers account. Study the platform.

Month 2: Create

Step 3: Brainstorm topics for your Udemy course (e.g., English, Writing, etc.) Key Ideas: What are you uniquely passionate about and can contribute to the world?

Step 4: Upload teaching materials that you've made to Teacher's Pay Teachers. Remember: You only need to use the materials.

Months 3-5: Reflect

Step 5: Keep track of your performance ratings. Read the feedback from customers.

Step 6: Plan to revise your content based on the valuable feedback that you receive.

Months 6-12: Revise and Refine

Step 7: Publish the revised content and add content, as necessary.

Step 8: Find new ideas and niches for a course and content creation.

Part 4: The 1,000,000+ CNY/Year Educator's Plan

	Year 1	Year 2	Year 3	Year 4	Year 5
Active Work	Training Center	School	School	School	School Or Own Business
Position	Teacher	Teacher	Middle Manager	Middle Manager	Senior Leader or Business Owner
Study or Experience	Teaching License	Leadership	Leadership	Leadership	Leadership
Qualifications Needed	Bachelor's degree	Teaching License	Experience	Experience Network building	Experience Network building
Income (CNY)	20,000/ month	30,000/ month	30,000/ month	40,000-50,000/ month	60,000-80,000+/ month
Passive Income Generation		Teachers Pay Teachers Udemy	Teachers Pay Teachers Udemy	Teachers Pay Teachers Udemy	Teachers Pay Teachers Udemy Copyright
Passive Income (CNY)		500/ month	1,000/ month	5,000/ month	15,000/ month

About the Author

Dr. William Clifton Green II is an educator, researcher, and startup founder who has been active in Shanghai, China for the past ten years. He has been pivotal in the creation of the Meiying Foreign Language Training Institute, which currently has 550 students and twenty-two members of staff. Under William's guidance, the center has expanded with two directly owned centers in Shanghai as well as a Franchise center in Pudong New District, which is also located in the city.

Over the past ten years, Dr. Green has been involved in Curriculum Development and teacher appraisal at Shanghai United International School. He has actively contributed to the *Week Ahead* educational newsletter organized by the nursery at Wellington College Bilingual Shanghai. The articles that he contributed were related to educational values, school-wide inclusion, and differentiated support for students. In addition, he has helped create IELTS test-prep content for City & Guild's online IELTS preparatory course. He is a certified IELTS examiner and has invigilated the exam at universities in China.

Dr. Green is also a certified K-12 teacher in the District of Columbia and has taught English in China, Japan, and the United States. Overall, William favors a more eclectic approach to language teaching, learning, and syllabus design. He believes that designing a syllabus should be, first and foremost, learner-centered.

Dr. Green is a language learning enthusiast. He has passed the level 5 HSK (Advanced Chinese proficiency exam). He has also passed the level 2 Japanese Language Proficiency Test. He speaks some Korean as well. He utilizes his experiences learning languages to support student language learning and development.

Dr. Green is a recent graduate of the Educational Leadership and Management program at Drexel University. His doctoral research focused on the use of technology in the classroom to promote Chinese junior high school students' language and twenty-first century skill development. As a result of this research, he is actively seeking to promote student language learning through utilizing technology that has been aligned to curricula objectives. He can be reached at williamgreenii@hotmail.com.

Dr. William Clifton Green II

www.ingramcontent.com/pod-product-compliance
Lightning Source LLC
Chambersburg PA
CBHW061331040426
42444CB00011B/2860